Fragile Environments

This book is due for return on or before the last date shown below.

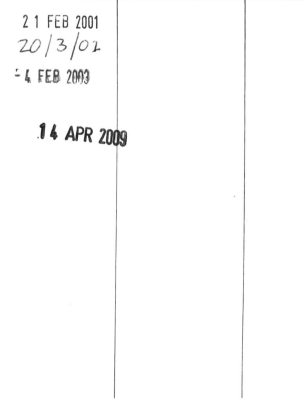

Other books of interest from Scottish Cultural Press

Fragile Environments

The Use and Management of Tentsmuir National Nature Reserve, Fife

Edited by
Graeme Whittington

SCOTTISH CULTURAL PRESS

First published 1996
Scottish Cultural Press
Unit 14, Leith Walk Business Centre
130 Leith Walk
Edinburgh EH6 5DT
Tel: 0131 555 5950
Fax: 0131 555 5018

British Library Cataloguing in Publication Data
A catalogue record for this book is available from the British Library

ISBN: 1 898218 77 3

Printed and bound by
BPC-AUP Aberdeen Ltd

Frontispiece: Aerial view of the Tentsmuir National Nature Reserve taken in 1990
(Cambridge University Collection of Air Photographs: copyright reserved)

Contents

This book is dedicated to Dr John Berry of Tayfield who has given a lifetime of interest to the welfare of Tentsmuir.

List of Illustrations

List of Tables

Preface

Graeme Whittington

The increasing encroachment of the built up area and, until recently, the taking of land into agricultural production has focused a great deal of attention on the need to conserve the rural landscape. The greater amount of leisure time available to people and the increased mobility accorded by widespread possession of the car have also furthered pressure on the rural area, especially those parts which might be classed as 'wildscapes'. Most concern associated with these matters has been voiced with regard to upland areas where the environment can be particularly fragile under continued human use and movement. Less attention has been given to lowland areas and especially to the coastal zones which possess large fringing sand dune systems, but they can be equally fragile.

In June 1994, a one day conference was held at Battleby, organised by the editor of this book for the Institute for Environmental History, University of St Andrews and sponsored by Scottish Natural Heritage, the South East Region of which has its headquarters at Battleby. The purpose of the conference was to draw together those people with an interest in conservation but especially those who shared concern over the fragile zones around our coasts. The area of Tentsmuir in north east Fife (Fig. 1) is an outstanding example not only of a large dune landscape, but one which is demonstrably suffering in many ways from the enormous pressures placed upon it by a number of conflicting landuses. The conference not only provided a platform for the airing of several specialists' views of the problems which exist on Tentsmuir and other similar shoreline areas in Britain, but also a forum for the discussion of the many points which those views generated. The papers given at the conference are presented here, with the exception of the one concerned with forestry, the main features of which are given in an Appendix. Chapter 5 is an invited addition to the proceedings. It was felt that an insight into the management methods, aims and problems that have been experienced through the time of the existence of the Tentsmuir National Nature Reserve would be valuable.

It needs to be emphasised that none of the chapters can be regarded as the definitive 'last word' about what has occurred. For example, there is seemingly disagreement over the rate of accretion being experienced on the shoreline, although this is largely a matter of the choice of points between which measurements are made. What this does highlight, however, is that rather than just concentrating on the linear extension of the coastline, research should be undertaken to ascertain the volume and variations in the volume of material which is accreting. There is also the matter of what the most appropriate future management for Tentsmuir should be. Several of the authors are in disagreement and the editor does not regard it as his prerogative to adjudicate between them. Lively and frank debate, rather than immediate prescription, was the purpose of the conference and of this book.

Perhaps the most important outcome of the conference was the appreciation shown by the large audience that areas like Tentsmuir do constitute a major and

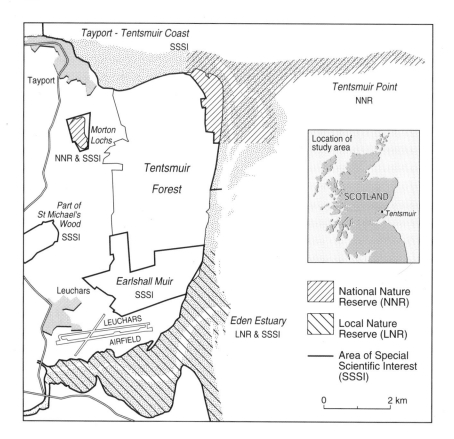

Figure 1: Tentsmuir: its location in Scotland and the areas designated for conservation, forestry and military use

multi-faceted problem. A basic feature arises from the question of what is being conserved? As Chapter 2 shows, areas like Tentsmuir have been evolving and changing over millennia. Does conservation merely mean the preservation of the landscape that exists today? Is change to be halted? Secondly, it is vital that plans, whatever they may be, consider the likelihood that conservation efforts may be in vain in an environment which is not only geomorphologically dynamic, as Chapter 1 reveals, but likely to become even more so if sea levels continue to rise at their present rate. Thirdly, there is the problem of conflicting demands placed upon such areas as Tentsmuir. How can the needs of birds, insects, foresters, recreation-seekers and farmers be accommodated within so small an area? As Chapter 4 demonstrates, the bird life on Tentsmuir today is in a sorry state compared with the not too distant past. Chapters 5 and 7 consider the management of the coastal zones but therein lies a further problem. The absence of a single statutory body to oversee and to manage the whole of an area such as Tentsmuir must surely render a solution to conflicting interests as being an unlikely, although desirable, aim. Scottish Natural Heritage, as a partial guardian of Tentsmuir but, more importantly, regarded by the general public as *the* protector of Scotland's unspoiled landscapes, must have a major role to play. The existence of a large land-holder in the shape of Forest Enterprise clearly means that its activities also have a vital bearing on the way ahead for areas such as Tentsmuir. Appendix 1 shows how Forest Enterprise see this future. A clear Plan has been put forward which, in essence, apart from the somewhat forbidding processes of its implementation, aims at ensuring and indeed claiming the resolving of conflicts. That will be of great importance for, as the following chapters show, there is much concern over the apparent divergence of interests as between the forester and the conservationist. The suggestion put forward in Chapter 7 that the way ahead is for SNH to 'promote integrated management…by stimulating understanding, co-operation and voluntary agreement among the range of users and statutory authorities by the creation of local fora', along with the avowed intentions of Forest Enterprise, provides the greatest hope that the damage already done to fragile environments, like that of Tentsmuir, might one day become a thing of the past. Whether that will also provide an answer to the thorny question as to what conservation should seek to be is another matter. It is also realistic to recognise that some changes which have created severe damage to the natural heritage interest in the past are now irreversible: no one can, and perhaps few would now wish to, remove the forestry plantation, nor is it realistic to expect a reduction in the pressure from recreational pursuits along the shore, although these two factors are mainly responsible for the loss of bird interest. On the other hand, certain changes could clearly take place, given the will and the finance to implement them. The whole question of water levels is critical here – Earlshall Muir, for example, could be transformed by more water. Conservationists, however, have also to decide on priorities; at Tentsmuir Point would it be justified to recreate, by intervention, the Great Slack for the exceptional botanical interest, if doing so interfered with the natural processes of geomorphological interest? As Chapter 6 indicates, there are strong feelings about the nature of management, not only with regard to the way it is carried out but also in relation to its overall aim. It was the intention of the symposium held at Battleby that all of the problems and attitudes aired there should be brought to the attention of as wide a public as possible. Areas like Tentsmuir are just as important in our national heritage as grand houses and conservation areas of towns.

Acknowledgements

Thanks are due to many people and organisations for making possible the holding of the original conference and for the subsequent publication of this book. Scottish Natural Heritage made their South Eastern Region Headquarters at Battleby available for the conference. North East Fife District Council and Fife Regional Council both gave grants towards publication costs. Graeme Sandeman from the School of Geography and Geology, University of St Andrews, produced the maps and diagrams which illustrate the various chapters. The Committee for Aerial Photography at the University of Cambridge gave permission to use the aerial views of Tentsmuir.

1

Sediment Accumulation Mechanisms on the Tentsmuir Coast

John McManus and Abhilasha Wal

Introduction

The rectangular 4 km by 8 km Tentsmuir area is a site of long-term nett accretion, with over 3.5 km of shoreline advance in 5000 years (Ferentinos & McManus 1981). Structurally it is composed mainly of two sequences of dune ridges with intervening slacks. The principal dune ridges are arranged approximately parallel to the nearby coast so that, in the north, bordering the Tay estuary they trend west-east, and on the coastlands of St Andrews Bay they trend north-south. At Tentsmuir Point, where the coastline turns from the open sea into the estuary the often rather poorly developed dunes are weakly aligned northwest-southeast. The 2–4 m high dunes and intervening 50–80 m wide inter-dune slack areas rest on a platform created by beach face accretion on the coast of St Andrews Bay.

In the Tentsmuir Point National Nature Reserve, where the mature dune systems are heath covered, the young dunes have *Ammophila* flourishing upon them. To seaward of the dunes are low gradient beaches which vary in width from 80 to 400 m. They are wider in the north and south and narrower and steeper in the centre, towards Kinshaldy. The lower foreshore typically shows ridge and runnel structures trending north-south, with widely spaced runnel openings facing east or northeast. The medium and fine sands form unbroken beach-faces with limited topographic expression, across which wind-blown sand travels freely.

To seaward, the bathymetry of St Andrews Bay is essentially a relatively simple downward slope, reaching the 20 m isobath 5–6 km offshore. In the north the Abertay Sands form the boundary between the Tay Estuary Channel and St Andrews Bay. They stretch eastwards for 6 km beyond Tentsmuir Point, providing an area of dangerous, shallow water more than 1 km in width, and incorporating a substantial island area in the southern entrance to Pool Channel.

The waters of St Andrews Bay are part of a macro-tidal system, with neap and spring tides exhibiting ranges of 3.5 m and 5 m respectively. The tidal currents in the open bay are relatively slow, exceeding 1 ms^{-1} only towards the mouths of the Eden and Tay Estuaries (Ferentinos & McManus 1981; Jarvis & Riley 1987; Al-Washmi 1995). The waters follow a clockwise rotating pattern on the rising tide and have an anticlockwise motion on the falling tide (Fig. 1.1). Towards the Tentsmuir Point area the rising tidal waters surge through the Pool Channel creating strong currents, often exceeding 2.5 ms^{-1}. The water flows have similar speeds but in the opposite direction during the early stages of the ebb tide. Here, and in the mouth of the Eden, substantial megaripple bedform systems are developed, especially on spring tides.

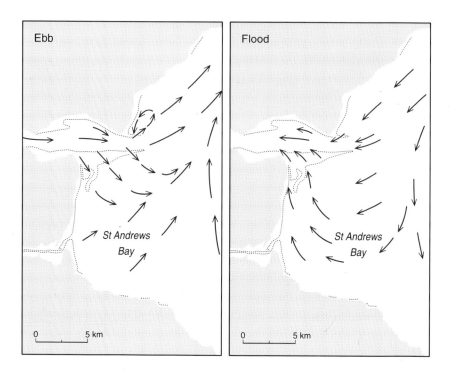

Figure 1.1: Tidal circulation patterns in St Andrews Bay

Beach Dynamic

The beach is that part of the coastal zone within which the most evident changes occur. Formerly it was thought that beach levels built up during the relatively calm
summer months, only to become eroded by wave activity during the winter (Davis
1983). However, in the last decade or so it has been recognised that the response is
much more complex (Carter 1986), and reference to wind records confirms that on
the North Sea coasts of Scotland, storm activity, with its associated erosive wave impact on beaches, is not confined to the winter months. Waves created by strong
winds in any season can drastically lower a beach face, and likewise rebuilding can
occur in any season. However, on balance, as will be shown later, strong, destructive
winds are more likely to occur in winter, and calm conditions in summer.

The beach system responds rapidly to changes in the wave or tidal conditions by
modification of the beach profile. Material removed from one part of the profile is
likely to become deposited elsewhere in the local system – up or down the beach
face – or more probably at some point along the shoreline.

Echo-sounding traverses at high water, repeated at two monthly intervals across
the margin of the Tay estuary tidal flats from Tayport to Tentsmuir Point and the
Abertay Sands between February 1971 and May 1972, were reported by McManus *et
al.* (1980). They showed that the margins of the northern beach area were very

stable, and that little change was detectable west of Tentsmuir Point. To the east of that point, at the northern end of Pool Channel, the profiles changed substantially through time, with a topography showing ridges and hollows with 4–5 m of relief in July 1971 which had become transformed into an essentially flat and featureless area by April 1972.

In June and July of 1990, Wal (1992) surveyed beach profiles at daily intervals using a Kern GKO-A automatic level on a total of eleven traverses of the Tentsmuir beaches. Two of the lines were on the northern shore and the remainder between Tentsmuir Point and the mouth of the Eden estuary. A traverse line east from the ice-house and tied to the SNH stile gate's square wooden post revealed no significant changes in the period 29.6.90 until 6.7.90 (Fig. 1.2), which coincided with the low tidal ranges around neap tide (Fig. 1.3a). However, between 7.7.90 and 13.7.90, as high tide levels rose from 4.5 m to 5.1 m, a middle beach-face ridge developed. This migrated to the top of the beach face by 23.7.90, on the peak of the spring tidal cycle, after which its separate identity became impossible to distinguish on a rather featureless beach. This line of profile was taken shoreward of the island in Pool Channel, where wave activity is restricted. Wind records from nearby RAF Leuchars for this period (Fig. 1.3b) show that until 13.7.90 the light winds were predominantly offshore and thereafter a significant proportion of onshore winds occurred as the local summer land- and sea-breeze system became established. The change in wind direction permitted stronger onshore wave activity which contributed to the changes in the beach profile, with accumulation of sand on the beach face and berm areas.

Similar patterns of change were observed on all profiles of the St Andrews Bay coastline measured during the same period. Thus during this single summer lunar tidal cycle there was a nett build up of sand along the North Sea shoreline of the Tentsmuir area.

The immediate source of sediment which is brought to the Tentsmuir area is the floor of St Andrews Bay, an area within which sediments have been deposited during late glacial and subsequent times (Browne & Jarvis 1983). In an analysis of the wave refraction patterns and the energy expended on the near shore and coastal margins, Sarrikostis and McManus (1987) demonstrated that wave fronts approaching the Fife coast from most directions become deformed in such a way that they sweep towards the Tentsmuir area. Consequently, as a result of the zig-zag progression of sand particles in response to waves breaking at an angle to the beach face, the waves approaching the coast from both north and south of the Tay therefore ensure transport of bed material not only shoreward from the bed of the embayment, but also northward along the shore, towards Tentsmuir Point.

Grain size analysis shows that the beach surface sediments coarsen from West Sands at St Andrews (0.17 mm) towards Tentsmuir Point (0.28 mm). Consequently, the beach face gradients generally increase northwards. At any one locality the sands become finer up the beach, so that beach face slopes also decrease landward. These fine to medium sands are highly susceptible to wind action, and sediment transport by wind is a very important feature of the upper foreshore and backshore zones, where the development of dune systems has led to the increase of vegetated land surface areas elevated above spring high water levels. At present active dune accumulations in the lee of the beaches are found extensively at Tentsmuir Point (2–4 m high), and to a limited extent at both Kinshaldy (1–2 m high) and West Sands, St Andrews (4 m high).

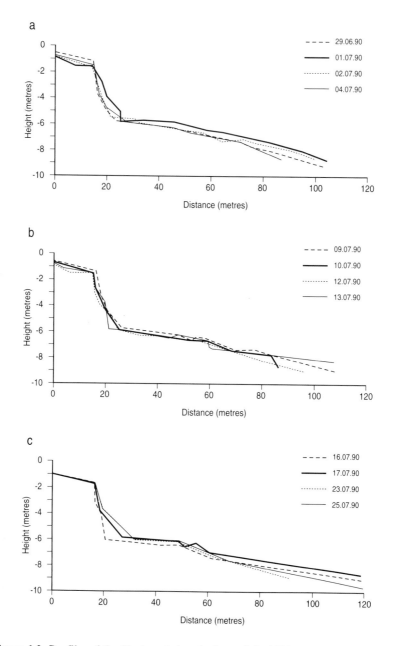

Figure 1.2: Profiles of the Tentsmuir beach; June–July 1990, east of the ice-house

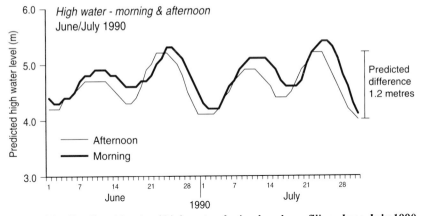

Figure 1.3a: Predicted levels of high water during beach profiling, June–July 1990

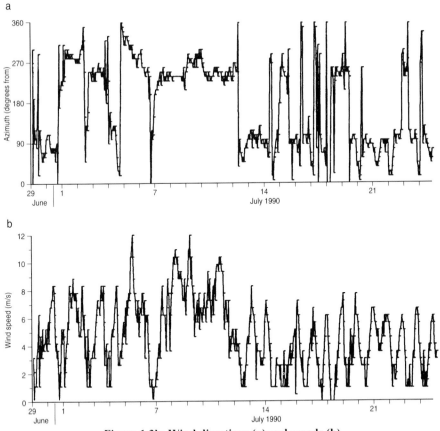

**Figure 1.3b: Wind directions (a) and speeds (b)
during the June–July 1990 beach profiling**

Growth of the Tentsmuir Point Area

The study of accretion at Tentsmuir Point has been documented by several workers, notably Grove (1950), Deshmukh (1974) and Wal (1992), all of whom relied upon analysis of sequential Ordnance Survey maps, Admiralty Charts, ground photographs and successive aerial photographs in the files of the SNH Cupar Office. The area is known to have been accreting in a north-eastward direction since 1812.

In the earliest documented growth phase, 1812–1854, the line of high water mark advanced on average north-eastwards by about 40 m, although there was an additional eastward projection in the south (Fig. 1.4). Although the area was well-known and frequently visited there is no further documentary evidence of the shoreline position until 1941 when there was construction of a line of anti-tank concrete blocks 'at high water mark'. Seaward of this line, and still visible today, a low ridge, known as the Defence Dune, was constructed also in 1941. The fact that it has survived until the present indicates that it, too, was close to or above high water level when it was built. Air photographs from 1948 suggest that a wide beach platform, approaching 500 m in width at Tentsmuir Point lay in front of the dunes at that time. By 1962 hummocky aeolian sand accumulations supporting pioneer vegetation (*Elymus farctus* and *Cakile maritima*) were present along the backshore, separated by narrow channels through which tidal waters occasionally penetrated on high water of spring tides. The line of dune growth had reached 40 m beyond the line of the Defence Dune. By 1972, the isolated hummocks had largely amalgamated so that a continuous vegetated 'land' area had been created, extending a further 25–30 m seawards. In front of this was a further series of mounds or 'islets' supporting pioneer plants.

Air photographs confirm that by 1978 these mounds had also become incorporated within the plant-colonised area suggesting an average dune margin advance of a further 60 m. A tidally flooded inlet penetrated this dune line, to the north of which further vegetated 'islets' had formed on the beach platform. To the east a 400 m long dune-covered spit, extending northwards from Tentsmuir Point, provided a substantial barrier to the penetration of North Sea waves. The 1984 air photographs reveal that the spit had broadened from 25 m to 80 m and the northern extremity had separated to create a recurved 'islet' over 300 m long on the platform. By 1990 the southern part of the spit and the 1978 'islets' had linked, and the northern 'islet' had greatly extended in all directions, although there remained a narrow tidal channel between it and the vegetated land area.

Overall, the vegetated land area at Tentsmuir Point advanced by 1 km in a northward direction and by 500 m eastwards between 1812 and 1990. In a north-eastward direction, perpendicular to the coastline, this amounts to a growth rate of 870 m in 178 years, or approximately 4.8 m annually. This very high rate of accretion has been achieved by retention of sand upon an already high platform area created in advance by the build up of beach materials. The average rise in the land level throughout the area, probably less than 2 m, has been greatly aided by entrapment of wind blown sand by the vegetation. In the past, the rate of accretion at Tentsmuir has been calculated on the basis that the 1941 line of concrete blocks marked the position of high water, rather than the contemporary line of the Defence Dune 80–160 m to seaward. By plotting the forward growth against time (Fig. 1.5), it is possible to see that, although accretion rates have certainly varied through time, the early pattern incorporating both the 1854 and defence dune data suggests a greater constancy in the

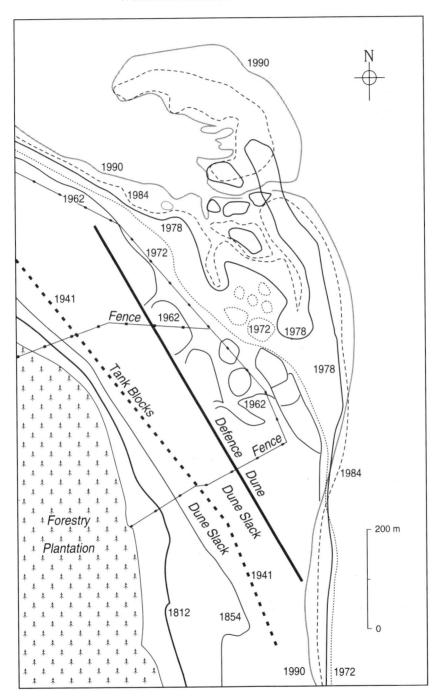

Figure 1.4: Known positions of high water mark at Tentsmuir from 1812 to 1990

rate of build up than that using the concrete block line. Using the former, a rate of 250 m per century is calculated, whereas using the latter gives a figure of 60 m per century. After 1941 the accretion rate increased greatly, with the development of the terminal hook to the headland, reaching rates of 1500 m per century. The overall longterm (178 year) rate of accretion measured in a north-easterly direction averages 4.8 m per year.

The growth of land at Tentsmuir Point involved the entrapment of sediment derived from elsewhere. Some of the sand was certainly derived from erosion of dunes by wave activity, and coastal erosion has been documented along different stretches of the Tentsmuir coast since 1964, notably north of Kinshaldy, but also at the southern end of the National Nature Reserve (NNR). Using a combination of air photographs and contoured maps constructed for the NNR in 1987, it is estimated that the volume of sediment accumulated at Tentsmuir Point between 1978 and 1990 was 33 x 10^3 m³. Similar analysis methods enable an estimation that 46 x 10^4 m³ of sand was eroded from the dune margins. Thus the coastal erosion on the Tentsmuir beaches to the south could have readily supplied the material accreted in the Point area.

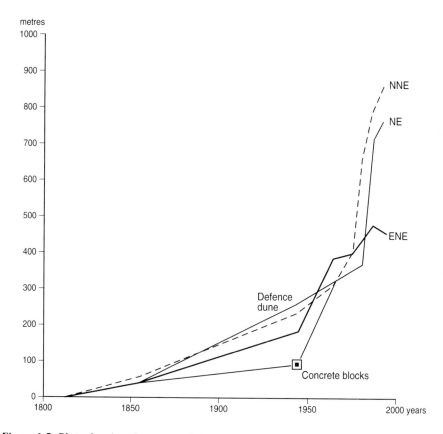

Figure 1.5: Plots showing the temporal changes in the position of the seaward edge of the dune system on a NE–SW line through Tentsmuir Point

Of the 500 m wide beach platform noted in 1948, over 300 m had been covered by dunes by 1990, and it is estimated that no more than 170 m of the plaform survives today. Because the area of accretion now lies very largely above the level of spring high water, the sediment covering the former beach platform must have been transported to the site by wind action, which therefore provides the second major constructive process contributing to the growth of land at Tentsmuir.

Long-Term Record of Winds at Tentsmuir

The nearest first class weather station to Tentsmuir Point is at RAF Leuchars, 9 km to the south, where records for over 70 years of measurement are available. Analysis of the wind information in Monthly Weather Reports of the Meteorological Office during the last 50 years has shown that there has been little change in the pattern of wind in the area during that period. A more detailed examination of measurements available for the period 1980–1990 confirms that the most prominent winds at Tentsmuir originated from the WSW, the next most common winds coming from the SSW. The south-westerlies (SSW–WSW sector) were the characteristic winds of the winter months of December, January and February. North-westerlies (NNW–WNW sector) were common only in March and April. Whilst the offshore winds blew for about 70 percent of the year, onshore winds blew for about 25 percent of the time. The onshore winds are prominent during the spring and autumn. They include easterlies and south-easterlies (ENE–SSE), dominantly the former.

During every month of the year, on average, winds of 5.6–8 ms^{-1} blew for 160–200 hours, with speeds of 8.6–10.7 ms^{-1} blowing for 90 hours a month in winter, 54 hours in spring and for only 26 hours in June and July, rising to 77 hours by October. Winds of 11–16.8 ms^{-1} were well represented from September (30 hrs) to March (61 hrs), being greatest during January (71 hrs). In summer such strong winds blew rarely, averaging 3–18 hours per month. Winds in excess of 17 ms^{-1} were generally experienced in December, January and March.

Offshore winds in winter blew for an average of 200 hours per month but decreased to 100–145 hours from April to July. The peak period for onshore winds was in April and May (140 hrs), but they were also significant in October (89 hrs) and February (2 hrs).

The land- and sea-breeze phenomenon is particularly well developed on this coast during periods of stable weather in early summer. The records show onshore breezes of 2–8 ms^{-1} rising to peak strengths in the evening, while the much gentler land breezes (never exceeding 1 ms^{-1}) typified night time and early morning. An example of the contrasting nature of the record of wind strengths and directions taken during a period of stable offshore winds, followed immediately by a period of land- and sea-breezes, is given in Figure 1.3b.

From the available data-base it is possible to construct wind roses to show the direction and strength of the wind during each month during the ten year analysis period (Wal & McManus 1993). The resultant patterns show either dominantly unimodal winds with offshore sense or onshore sense or bimodal, in which the winds were sometimes onshore and sometimes offshore. Thus three subgroups of conditions may be recognised; bimodal but dominantly onshore; bimodal but dominantly offshore, or bimodal with equal onshore and offshore. In addition there can also be a unimodal longshore wind and a bimodal which possesses a longshore element.

Sand Movement in Response to Wind

It is a common observation that sand is blown across the beach during periods of high wind and that little motion occurs in relatively calm weather. In order to determine the rates of sand motion, a series of tubular traps (Leatherman 1978) were emplaced on the beach either individually in different sub-environments, or in clusters to obtain statistical information on the variability of the quantities entrapped locally under different conditions. Each trap was carefully inserted into the beach face or dune surface with the entry slit flush to the ground level and pointing towards the direction of the oncoming wind. The trap was opened for 15 minutes, the entrapped material was bagged, returned to the laboratory for weighing, drying at 110°C, and reweighing to determine the percentage of moisture in the blown sands. A vertical array of cup anemometers was arranged at 0.5 m, 1.5 m, and 2.0 m above the ground surface during deployment of the traps, so that the shear velocity of the wind at the ground surface could be calculated. During active sand transport shear velocities of 0.19 ms^{-1} to 0.52 ms^{-1} were calculated from wind profiles which recorded speeds of 4 ms^{-1} to 20 ms^{-1} at a height of 2 m above the beach surface.

The rates of sand entrapment varied from location to location on the beach (Fig. 1.6). The greatest figures were obtained from the middle of the beach face ($0.01–0.3$ kgs^{-1}m^{-1}) when shear velocities of $0.2–0.46$ ms^{-1} were recorded. The rates of transport decreased both up and down the beach, to $0.08–0.16$ kgs^{-1}m^{-1} on the upper beach and $0.019–0.03$ kgs^{-1}m^{-1} on the lower beach face. Vegetation greatly reduces wind speeds and surface shear stresses so that very little sediment passed behind the first vegetated dune ridges. The sediment is rapidly deposited as the wind enters the vegetated dune system.

The source of sediment for the wind may exert a limiting influence on the quantities of sand available for transport by the wind. Offshore winds may deflate the dune system, as well as the upper, middle and lower beach face areas, as they blow across commonly no more than a few hundred metres of the coastal zone. The longshore winds may blow along several kilometres of dry upper beach face and therefore have a greater potential for removal and transport of sand. Onshore winds will entrain any dry sand on the beach face, but the sands of this sector of the beach are tidally wetted, and those most freely available are above high water mark.

Thus the source limitation, the presence of moisture and the presence of vegetation all serve as additional constraints to wind entrainment and transport of sand particles.

Sand Transport Potential

Direct observation of sand in motion confirms the conditions and limits under which movement will occur. The long term wind speed and direction data may be used to calculate the quantities of sand which could be moved under each set of conditions. An expression derived by Fryberger and Dean (1979) enables the excess of the measured wind speed above a threshold speed (5.9 ms^{-1}), below which the $0.25–0.3$ mm diameter sand grains will not move, and the duration of the wind to be employed

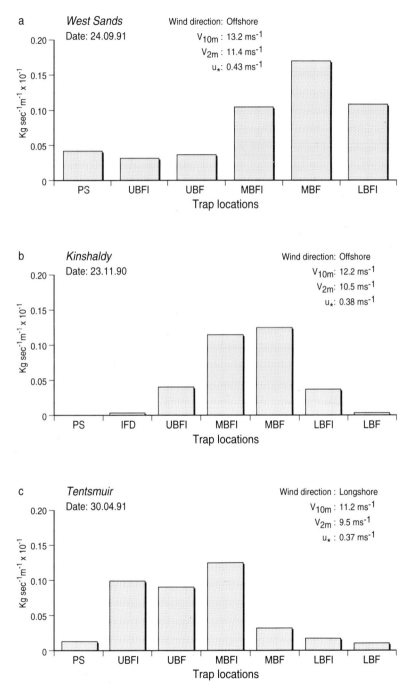

Figure 1.6: Rates of entrapment of sand at various positions on the Tentsmuir foreshore and dune system

in this calculation:

$$Q \propto t \, [V^2 - (V - Vt)]$$

where V is the wind velocity at 10 m, Vt is the threshold velocity for sand motion, and t is the duration of wind recording. Q is the potential sand drift which is normally quoted in vector units (VU) to underline that the quantities are moving in specific directions determined by the wind.

From the VU figures derived, Wal & McManus (1993) constructed ten-year average monthly sand roses in a manner analogous to that used in forming wind roses, but now indicating the quantities and directions of motion of sand for each month of the year at Tentsmuir. Like the wind roses described earlier, the sand roses also show unimodality and bimodality with onshore, offshore or alongshore sense of motion.

During the period October to the end of January, strong *offshore, unimodal* winds show very high potential seaward sand transport (700–3000 VU).

During the period February to the end of June, rather weaker *unimodal onshore* winds yield lower potential sand transport (from 855 VU in March to 197 VU in June).

Offshore dominant bimodal winds may occur at any time of the year, particularly September to the end of December, but also in spring. Potential transport is substantial (400–800 VU).

Onshore dominant bimodal winds are less common than their offshore counterparts but normally occur in spring (April and May) and late winter (January and February). The potemtial sand transport is very variable from year to year (104–800 VU).

The *balanced bimodal* winds with almost equal onshore and offshore components characterise the summer months (June to the end of August), when low transport potential is normal (25–74 VU).

Northward directed longshore winds, which occur mainly in winter, show variable potential sand transport (110–1700 VU). Southward longshore winds are rare.

The patterns summarised above are no more than long term generalisations. Onshore or longshore transport may occur during periods normally associated with offshore transport as a result of the actions of atypical weather systems. In some years the coast will experience far more strong winds than during others, so that annual sediment budgets or sand motion will vary greatly from year to year. It is important to note that the numerical values provided for the vector units are computed on the basis of free availability of dry sand on all occasions on which the threshold conditions are exceeded. In consequence, they are over-estimates, as no allowance can be made for periods of wet, windy weather (not common in an area receiving 500–600 mm of rain annually), nor are allowances made for the stage of the tide in relation to areas of exposed sand on the beach. However, in all cases the same considerations of variability hold true for this coast, so that the figures for vector units should be treated as relative rather than as absolute values.

Each of the major wind directions (onshore or offshore) is associated with distinctive groups of bedforms developed by the particles as they cease their motion.

Onshore winds give rise to intermittent and discontinuous movement of sand grains on the drier parts of the foreshore, especially the upper beach face and the zone above high water. The beach face becomes an active zone of deflation in the lower and middle sectors and accretion in the upper beach and foredune areas. Many particles are driven toward the back beach and beyond into the dunes, their movement often being observed as patches of mobile dry sand blowing as units across a stable substrate of damp sand. Sediments entering the dune belt are likely to be deposited behind the landward pointing lee dune or to become entrapped by the vegetation.

Offshore winds also generate intermittent movement in the initial stages of development. The sediment is carried across the bare sand surfaces of the non-vegetated dunes, often creating mobile ripples. The beach face suffers deflation as the sand is swept in mobile strips across and down the beach face and onto the damp area beside the water line. In this zone much of the sand becomes entrapped to form adhesion ripples, which grow slowly into the direction from which the wind is blowing. Because the sand is moved as a saltating mass, many of the grains leap across the damp zone to pass directly into the seawater offshore. Within the dune belt the sand may become built up into mobile dunes in the form of small barchanoid structures and it is only these winds which lead to the formation of small (less than 1 m high) foredune ridges in the wind shadow of the main dune front and slightly seaward of it, at the back of the beach.

Longshore winds blow north along the beach face, carrying dry sand particles as clusters, often as clouds which sweep discontinuously across the exposed sands. Deflation is widespread, and rippled surfaces form on strips of mobile sand on the upper beach and foredune areas. Accumulations in wind shadow areas, behind flotsam, shell fragments or isolated grass tussocks, are common.

Conclusion

On any coast the long-term pattern of changes showing nett accretion or loss of sediment is the outcome of the integrated impacts of several natural processes acting in concert. The Tentsmuir coastline is no exception to this concept.

It has been demonstrated that wave activity in St Andrews Bay carries sediments towards the head of the embayment through refraction of the shoaling wave fronts. The northward sense of movement of the waves along the Tentsmuir coast serves to encourage a normal progression of sediment along the beach face towards Tentsmuir Point. The long-term continuation of this supply of sediment has been to create a beach built platform protected behind the offshore Abertay Sands and associated islands and which has extended north-eastwards, partially filling the formerly navigable shipping lane of Pool Channel.

A second set of processes controlled by wind activity has acted simultaneously. It has been demonstrated here that the commonest, offshore winter winds may carry sand from the dunes to create wind shadow foredunes at the back of the upper beach. They also blow sand onto the lower beach and into nearshore tidal waters. The tidal waters recycle the sands to the beach as part of their natural activity, so that the principal substantial geomorphological impact of the offshore winds lies in the production of shadow foredunes. Onshore winds, common in spring and autumn, serve to transport sand up the beach face, to enhance incipient foredune growth, and to carry limited quantities of sand into the dune systems beyond the beach. Exceptionally strong onshore winds in February 1966 and March 1981 are known to have been associated with unusually heavy accretion of sand at Tentsmuir (Nature Conservancy

Council Warden's Reports). Longshore winds from the south may carry very large volumes of sand along the coast towards Tentsmuir Point. On one weekend in November 1968 a group of sedimentologists visiting the area to examine the inter-relationships between the beach and dune sediments encountered severe longshore transport during which continuous sheets of sand more than waist deep blew along the coast for at least three hours. On the following day, when the wind had dropped, the platform area at Tentsmuir Point hosted a swarm of barchan dunes reaching up to 1 m in height. It was calculated that as a result of that one storm more than 40,000 tonnes of sand were transported to Tentsmuir Point. Some, and not necessarily the bulk of the material remained above high tide level, but much of the material was swept north into the channel of the Tay Estuary, perhaps to become recycled into St Andrews Bay in the course of time. Thus, not everything which is transported to-wards the Point will become entrapped in the dunes.

The northeastward growth of the Tentsmuir Point area at a rate of over 4.8 m per year has been sustained for at least the last 178 years. Fresh dunelands are being pro-vided constantly for care and nurture by Scottish Natural Heritage, in one of its genuinely appreciating assets. If present conditions are maintained there is every reason to anticipate that growth will continue, but, if the foreseen global rise of sea level does materialise during the next century there is no guarantee that sedimenta-tion will continue in this area, and then accretion may give way to erosion. It is nec-essary to recognise the first signs of such change and plan for such an eventuality.

Bibliography

Al-Washmi, H A, 'St Andrews Bay: a sedimentological, geophysical and morphological study' (Ph.D. thesis, University of St Andrews, 1995)
Browne, M A E and Jarvis, J, 'Late Devensian marine erosion in St Andrews Bay, east-central Scotland', *Quaternary Newsletter,* 41 (1983), pp. 11–17
Carter, R W G, *Coastal Environments* (Academic Press, 1988), p. 617
Davies, R A Jnr., *Depositional systems: a genetic approach to sedimentary geology* (Prentice-Hall Inc., Engelwood Cliff, New Jersey, 1983), p. 669
Deshmukh, I J, 'Fixation, accumulation and release of energy by Ammophila arenaria, Tentsmuir' (Ph.D. thesis, University of Dundee, 1974)
Ferentinos, G and McManus, J, 'Nearshore processes and shoreline development in St Andrews Bay, Scotland, UK', *Holocene Marine Sedimentation in the North Sea Basin,* ed. Nio, S D, Shittenhelm, R T E and van Weering, T C E (Special Publication, International Association of Sedimentologists, 5, 1981), pp. 161–74
Fryberger, S H and Dean, G, 'Dune forms and wind regime', *A Study of Global Sand Seas,* ed. McKee, E D (US Geological Survey Professional Paper, 1979), no. 1052, pp. 137–69
Grove, A T, 'Tentsmuir – Fife. Soil Blowing and Coastal Changes' (Unpublished Manuscript, Nature Conservancy Council, Edinburgh, 1950), p. 24
Jarvis, J and Riley, C A R, 'Sediment transport in the mouth of the Eden Estuary', *Estuarine, Coastal & Shelf Science,* 24 (1987), pp. 463–81
Leatherman, S P, 'A new aeolian sand trap design', *Sedimentology,* 25 (1978), pp. 303–6
McManus, J, Buller, A T and Green, C D, 'Sediments of the Tay Estuary: VI Sediments of the lower and outer reaches', *Proceedings of the Royal Society of Edinburgh,* 78B (1980), pp. 133–53
Sarrikostis, E and McManus, J, 'Potential longshore transports on the coasts north and south of the Tay Estuary', *Proceedings of the Royal Society of Edinburgh,* 92B (1987), pp. 297–310

Wal, A, 'Sedimentological effects of aeolian processes active in the Tentsmuir area, Fife, Scotland' (Ph.D. thesis, University of St Andrews, 1992)

Wal, A and McManus, J, 'Wind regime and sand transport on a coastal beach-dune complex: Tentsmuir, Eastern Scotland', *The Dynamics and Environmental Context of Aeolian Sedimentary Systems*, ed. Pye, K (Geological Society Special Publication, 1993), no. 72, pp. 59–172

2

Landuse on Tentsmuir:
A History of Diverse Activities

Graeme Whittington

'...one comes forth on Tents Moor, a waste and empty territory, a land of Lost
Footsteps... no one can enter it without feeling he has penetrated a region
apart...'

Geddie, 1927

Introduction

Sand dune areas of any great extent have, through time, witnessed periods of both
exploitation and almost total abandonment but seldom have they been the focus, as
today, of so many conflicting uses. Tentsmuir is no exception to this. Through the
ages, it can be seen as a mirror which not only reflects the value which humans put
upon such areas, but also as showing a strong relationship with the different levels of
technology that have been available to our societies through time.

The Earliest Exploitation

The clearest knowledege we have of the earliest exploitation of Tentsmuir, dating to
the seventh millennium bp (before present), comes from the work of Coles (1971)
who excavated the Mesolithic site at Morton. Here was a community which was
very dependent upon the natural environment for its sustenance. The halfway house
provided by Tentsmuir, by dint of its location between the sea and 'solid land', gave
this early group of hunters and gatherers the best of different worlds; within close
proximity there were several habitats which could be exploited – the sea for fish, the
inshore area for shellfish, the wet, sandy zone for birds and eggs and the extensive
forested region inland for vegetable products and animals. Artefactual evidence
shows that all of these habitats were exploited, while the occupied site seems to have
been in a wooded area as faunal evidence not only indicates the presence of shade
but also of fallen timber (Coles 1983).

Tentsmuir continued to be attractive throughout the prehistoric period when tech-
nological levels were at a primitive stage. The light, sandy soils of the zone behind
the fronting dunes may have been low in nutrients and may have suffered from
sandblow but they were eminently suitable at a time when the ard provided the high
point in cultivation technology. Thus, it is no surprise that evidence has been found
for settlement in the area, in the shape of both Neolithic and Bronze age pottery on
Earlshall Muir.

The advent of the mouldboard plough enabled farmers to turn their attention to heavier soils while also perhaps causing a shift in emphasis as to the agricultural value of sandy areas. Over much of Tentsmuir, however, at varying depths below the present land surface, there is an extensive layer of charcoal-impregnated, humic sand. This layer has been examined by means of pollen and soil-fabric analyses. It would appear that the charcoal layer relates to a former land surface on which systematic muir burning was practised over a long period. The pollen record shows the area to have supported a heath in which *Calluna vulgaris* (heather) was dominant but that, probably due to injudicious burning, this was eventually replaced by Poaceae (grasses). The charcoal and pollen records (Fig. 2.1) suggest that Tentsmuir was being exploited as a managed pasture (Gimingham 1971) and a radiocarbon date indicates that this was occurring during the sixth century AD. Today, on the eastern margin of Tentsmuir, there exists a farmsteading with the name of Pitlethie. The element *pit* in this name is indicative of a Pictish presence in this area (Whittington 1977) and it is probable that the muir burning revealed in the sand zone provides evidence for a pastoral activity which complemented an arable agriculture on the silty soils lying inland of the sands. Just as the Mesolithic people exploited the ecotonal nature of the Tentsmuir area so the Picts or their predecessors took advantage of two areas with differing agricultural potential.

In a sense, Tentsmuir might be regarded as having, during the Pictish period, become marginalised in terms of human exploitation. That, however, would be a mistaken view, because, right up to the time of the agricultural improvement movement in the eighteenth century, the pasturing of cattle played a vital and integral part in land management and farming practice. It could well be that the use to which Tentsmuir was put at this time shows not only human response to changing technology but also the capacity for exploiting a new situation. One other effect was to alter drastically the floral composition on the sands (Fig. 2.1).

The Seventeenth Century

Unfortunately Scotland has no equivalent of England's Domesday Book, so further knowledge of the human exploitation of Tentsmuir is denied until the advent of mapping when the area was first depicted in Blaeu's Atlas (Fig. 2.2). That was published in the mid-seventeenth century but probably records the landscape as it appeared in the late sixteenth century. By this time, it seems that the farm at Pitlethie was accompanied by other dwellings named as Shanwell, East and West Fetters, Bridgend, Guhyt Croft and Nethermore. It is noticeable, however, that these all tend to lie at the inner margin of the sand zone. This was perhaps due to the severely water-logged nature of much of Tentsmuir at this time. Besides the two small lochs in the south, there are two others, one near West Fetters and the other south of Bridgend. Most prominent, however, is the very large Moss-myre, sharing the same water symbol as the lochs, which lies to the east of Leuchars and Craigie. It thus has the appearance of a vast loch on the map but is more likely to be one of the large dune slacks which would have flooded very easily. At that time, the shore would probably have lain further to the west than it does now which would have induced a higher water table. That the area was exceedingly wet is shown by the placename Leuchars – originating probably at the time when Gaelic was the local tongue and

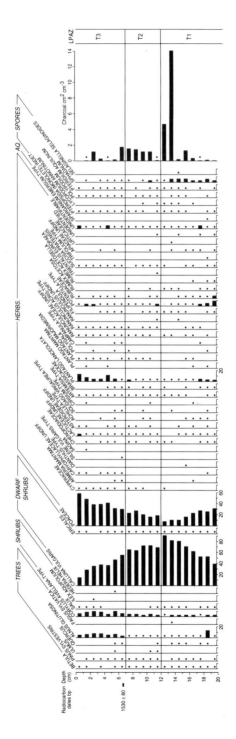

Figure 2.1: A pollen diagram from a buried charcoal layer on Tentsmuir

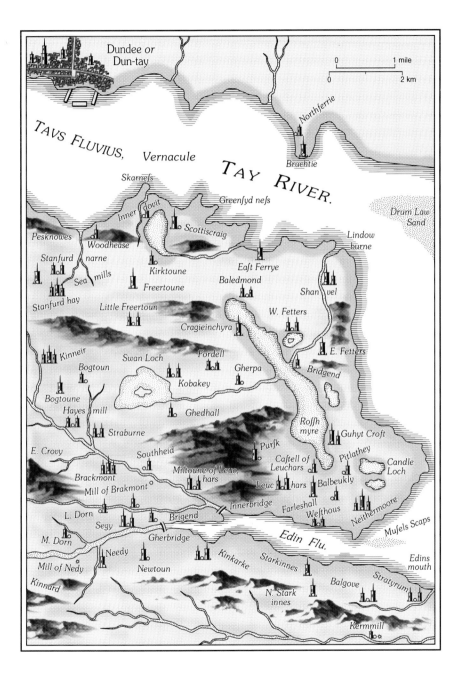

Figure 2.2: Tentsmuir in the late sixteenth century as depicted in Blaeu's Atlas

indicating the existence of a rush-covered, wet area.

The Eighteenth Century

The Statistical Account for Scotland records at the end of the eighteenth century, for Leuchars parish alone, an area of 36 acres to the south and west of the settlement which was 'covered with water to a considerable depth in the winter season, and not free from water in summer' (Kettle 1796: 586). The same author records the existence of '4 long, broad, beautiful, and almost parallel canals' which he names as Canal-loch (the Candle Loch of Blaeu?), White-Myre, Toremont, and Tents-muir, or Big Waters.

The map coming from Roy's Military Survey of the mid-eighteenth century (Fig. 2.3) might shed further light on the Tentsmuir of this period although his recording of information is notoriously random (Whittington & Gibson 1986). There is no sign of Blaeu's pseudo-loch or the canals named by Kettle but it is known that an attempt, by means of a three mile long cutting, was made in the early eighteenth century to drain the moorland on Leuchars Estate. Roy's map may, therefore, show how successful that was, especially if the survey was undertaken in the summer when water in dune slacks, the most likely explanation for Kettle's canals, could have been minimal. What is learnt from Roy's map, however, is that farming communities appear at that time to be more numerous. Fermtouns have now penetrated beyond the inner margins of Tentsmuir. Apart from Morton, none of the other settlements is named. They do, however, have the typical appearance of farming communities of the time with their ridged infields and kailyards. They do not allow any inferences to be made about possible population totals as the settlements are shown in a purely symbolic form.

Some thirty years after Roy's map came that of Ainslie and it contains considerably more detail (Fig. 2.4). Whether settlement, and consequently landuse, had intensified, as suggested by Ainslie's map, is not certain but it is certainly conceivable. More land for farming could have been available, as the *Statistical Account* (Kettle 1796: 586) records the enlarging of the existing drain in the late eighteenth century. This so-called Great Drain was twenty feet wide and fourteen feet deep and apparently the farmers were growing, with some success, a wide range of crops – oats, barley, wheat, rye, flax, clover, turnips, potatoes and cabbage. This success was also in no small measure due to the liberal application of lime, brought into the area by sea and from local lime kilns. The compiler of the Leuchars Parish account eulogised:

> It is not easy to describe the pleasure in viewing luxuriant crops, adorning the place where the eye had been accustomed to see stagnant water and noxious vapour impregnated with diseases and death. (Kettle 1796: 587)

Even at the time of his writing, the majority of Tentsmuir was given over to rough grazing on the dunes; cattle were pastured but the main users were sheep. According to the *Statistical Account* (Kettle 1796: 590) 1940 were pastured on some 2500 ha.

The intensive drainage activities on Tentsmuir would not only have done much to change its appearance but the concomitant alterations to its floral and faunal habitats must have been far reaching.

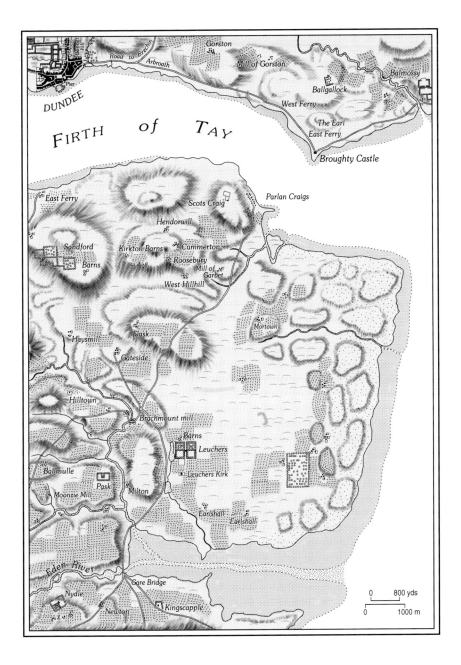

Figure 2.3: Tentsmuir *c.* 1750, according to Roy's Military Survey
(Redrawn from Roy's Military Survey (K. TOP. XLVIII-25-A). By permission of the British Library)

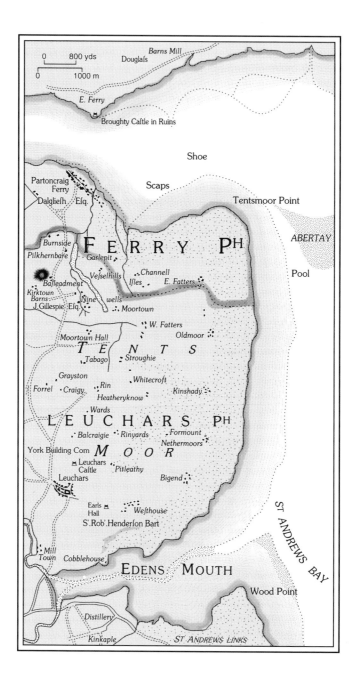

Figure 2.4: Tentsmuir towards the end of the eighteenth century as mapped by Ainslie

The Nineteenth Century

Despite the drainage that had been undertaken, there were still six lochs in existence on Tentsmuir, reported as being 'very long and very narrow, running parallel to each other, and between these moors and the adjacent country' (Brown 1822). Candle Loch was said to be the deepest and longest, hence the probable reason for it alone being named on the earliest map. The only other loch which is named seems to be the Toremont of earlier authors but it was then called, like the farmsteading nearby, Foremunt.

The nineteenth century saw a new phase of land occupation occurring on Tentsmuir Farm. Engrossment had become, by 1836, the order of the day on Tentsmuir, and its effect is recorded in the *New Statistical Account:*

> Tentsmoor, which of old used to be studded with turf built cottages, and gardens and crofts attached to them, is now, in great measure, depopulated, from the extensive farms which have been formed upon it. (Watson 1845: 223)

The effect of this was to cause Tentsmuir to take on an appearance which can still be seen, in part, today. The western zone, as attested by the first edition of the Ordnance Survey six inch maps, was worked from single-tenant farmsteadings. The eastern half, however, had changed. Few farmsteadings were left and even these were to disappear at a later date. With depopulation, the drains were neglected and bogs became more extensive; furthermore, the newly extended farms were running more sheep on the dunelands and injudicious muir burning led, as it had in the Dark Ages, to the demise of heather and its replacement by coarse grasses.

In the last decade of the nineteenth century, the eastern part of Tentsmuir was described as 'a large tract of barren moorland... fit for nothing but harbouring rabbits, a species of stock once in great repute, but now nearly extirpated' (Berry 1894: 225) – a condition in which it would stay for many years. In a sense the area had come full circle but far from its original nature.

The Planning Era

It might be considered that the drain digging and liming of the land provide the first examples of land management and landuse planning on Tentsmuir. The late nineteenth century saw this extended. Between 1876 and 1940, the Shanwell area in the north was devoted to grouse (Berry 1894). Heather was transplanted into the area by means of sods cut elsewhere on Tentsmuir, grouse were brought in from Perthshire and carefully controlled burning ensured healthy conditions for the birds. The central area, in which some arable farming had continued, also changed in nature. The land was laid down to grass and the tenant farmers raised cattle there, with supplementary grazing on the dunes (Smith 1905).

Recognition of the importance of Tentsmuir as an area which possessed great floral and faunal riches, led to large areas being singled out for conservation. Morton Lochs (1952) and Tentsmuir Point (1954) were declared National Nature Reserves and both areas were subsequently added to and notified as Sites of Special Scientific Interest (SSSI). Earlshall Muir (1955) and St Michael's Wood (1971) also gained SSSI status (see Appendix 2). Thus another strand of interest and of potential control was imposed upon the already complex situation on Tentsmuir.

Thus the area underwent a further change from its once natural state, but that event paled into insignificance compared with one in 1924 when the Government purchased most of the eastern part of Tentsmuir for forestry. By 1927, 700 ha had been put under *Pinus sylvestris* and *Pinus nigra*. By 1954, this had increased to nearly 1500 ha. The open zone of Tentsmuir was thus severely reduced. This was to be taken much further by the establishment of the Leuchars Royal Air Force Station in 1917 and its absorption of two farms in the period 1918–1939, with further extensions occurring during the period of the Second World War.

The greater mobility and leisure time now possessed by the general population have also furthered the catalogue of landuses to which Tentsmuir has been put. The varied nature of this area with its pinewoods, heathland and seashore has attracted people to undertake such diverse activities as walking, mountain-biking, bird-watching and beachcombing. In order to ensure a minimum of danger to this fragile environment, cars are confined to specially designated areas but this in itself has enabled more people to visit the area. The current mixture of Forest Enterprise (formerly Forestry Commission) controlled land, Sites of Special Scientific Interest, Nature Reserves, commercial farming and leisure activities indicate that the comment made at the beginning of this chapter regarding Tentsmuir being the focus of many conflicting uses is well made.

Conclusion

The landuse history of Tentsmuir has been extremely varied over time. Conflicts of interest certainly surfaced in the middle of the nineteenth century when the agricultural improving movement disrupted the lives of many smallholders. Such conflicts have, however, intensified with further changes in technology and society. Furthermore, it has to be recognised that what exists on Tentsmuir today is the result of hundreds of years of human activity, not the least of which has been the introduction of rabbits. It is possible to preserve what exists now, by means of judicious planning, or the emergence of a continually changing landscape could be allowed as new uses and demands affect the area. This is a situation which is not confined to Tentsmuir but also involves other fragile sand environments, especially those which lie in close proximity to large centres of population. Who makes the decision as to what should take place in these fragile zones is another matter, but upon them lies the responsibility of deciding whether areas such as Tentsmuir remain memorials of millennia of evolution, fossilised at the end of the twentieth century, or whether future generations should be allowed to record a continuing history of landuse change.

Bibliography

Berry, W, 'On the introduction of grouse to the Tentsmuir in Fife', *Annals of Scottish Natural History*, 12 (1894), pp. 197–203

Brown, W, 'An account of Sheuchy Dyke, in the East of Fife', *Archaeologia Scotica*, II (1822), pp. 192–8

Coles, J M, 'The early settlement of Scotland: excavations at Morton, Fife', *Proceedings of the Prehistoric Society*, 37 (1971), pp. 284–366

Coles, J M, 'Morton Revised', *From the Stone Age to the 'Forty-Five*, O'Connor, A M and Clarke, D V (John Donald, Edinburgh, 1983), pp. 9–18

Geddie, J, *The Fringes of Fife* (Chambers, Edinburgh, 1927)

Gimingham, C H, 'British heathland ecosystems: the outcome of many years of management by fire', *Proceedings of the Tenth Annual Tall Timbers Fire Ecology Conference* (1971), pp. 293–321

Kettle, M, 'Parish of Leuchars', *The Statistical Account of Scotland*, ed. Sinclair, Sir John (Edinburgh, 1796), pp. 585–607

Smith, W G, 'Botanical Survey of Scotland: Forfar and Fife', *Scottish Geographical Magazine,* 21 (1905), pp. 57–83

Watson, D, 'Parish of Leuchars', *The New Statistical Account of Scotland*, IX (1845), pp. 217–29

Whittington, G, 'Placenames and the settlement pattern of Dark Age Scotland', *Proceedings of the Society of Antiquaries of Scotland*, 106 (1977), pp. 99–110

Whittington, G and Gibson, A J S, *The Military Survey of Scotland: A Critique* (Historical Geography Research Series, 18, 1986)

3

Invertebrate Populations:
Management for Survival?

Pete Kinnear

Introduction

Britain has a long coastline and a variety of habitats influenced by the sea. These coastal areas contain many of our rarest invertebrates and many rich and interesting invertebrate communities. Coastal habitats are typically characterised by low and open-structured vegetation – limited by exposure, salt water and spray – together with eroding or accreting substrata which usually ensure large areas of bare surfaces. The varied vegetation structure and bare ground are inherent features of many coastal sites important for the survival of rich invertebrate faunas. Most coastal invertebrates are confined to specific coastal habits. However, species characteristic of other open areas – heaths, grasslands and ruderal sites – also share coastal areas. As natural inland habitats are altered, so coastal areas may become even more vital as refuges for these more generalist species. Excluding the microscopic species, the British invertebrate fauna comprises about 30,000 species. Insects make up just over three quarters of this number.

Tentsmuir has long been a focus for naturalists, both amateur and professional. There are botanical descriptions and detailed plants lists from about 1840 onwards (e.g. Balfour 1902; Crapper 1940, 1956, 1957; Crawford & Wishart 1966; Gimingham 1964; Howie 1884; Ingram 1968; Poore 1954; Robertson 1915; Shaw 1935; Smith & Smith 1905; West 1910). Surprisingly, despite the Victorian mania for bug hunting, there is a paucity of comparable invertebrate recording.

Invertebrate Recording

Identification of most insect species is often difficult and there are many critical groups which require expert determination. Only a small number of groups has been studied. In the 1960s a group from Dundee University began detailed ecological studies of the sand dune arthropods on Tentsmuir Point NNR (Cotton 1971; Cotton & Miller 1974; Deshmukh 1974) and made a general description of the invertebrate fauna (Cotton 1968). In the period 1963–67 extensive collecting of beetles and bugs was carried out by the reserve warden, Malcolm Smith (Smith 1971a). A detailed ecological study was made of the spider fauna in 1966 (Duffey 1968).

In the mid 1970s the potential threat to soft coasts from the development of North Sea Oil provided an incentive for the Nature Conservancy Council (NCC) to contract the Institute of Terrestrial Ecology (ITE) to undertake a systematic survey of both the vegetation and invertebrates of many of Scotland's sand dunes, including Tentsmuir. Information was urgently needed to ensure that on-shore installations were sited where they would cause the least damage to wildlife (Welch 1989).

Groups of invertebrates which have been looked at in some detail on some parts of Tentsmuir are, with the exception of spiders (Aranae), mostly insects and include the beetles (Coleoptera), bugs (Hemiptera), butterflies and moths (Lepidoptera) and dragonflies (Odonata).

A brief summary of the findings is given here highlighting those species which are assessed as scarce or have limited distributions and may therefore be considered potentially vulnerable or deserving of consideration in conservation management.

a) Beetles – Coleoptera

Over 460 species of beetle have been recorded, although collecting has almost exclusively been confined to the National Nature Reserves at Tentsmuir Point and Morton Lochs and a small part of Earlshall. Most of the recording was carried out between 1963 and 1971 (Smith 1971b), although there has been some survey work since (Dodd 1979; Foster 1988).

Forty-one species (9 percent), (Table 3.1a) are classified as having Red Data Book (RDB), Notable or Habitat Indicator Species status according to the Invertebrate Site Register (Ball 1986). Two species are classed RDB Category 3 – Rare: *Arena tabida*, which has been found on the front dunes at the south east corner of Tentsmuir forest, and *Pissodes validirostris*, a species which inhabits pine cones and would normally be associated with native pinewoods. At present the latter species is only known from the long established plantation at Fir Park on the Earlshall Site of Special Scientific Interest (SSSI), where two other native pinewood indicator species are also known, *Magdalis duplicta* and *M. phlegmatica*. While these occurrences are of interest they should not deflect attention away from the importance of species from open habitats.

Fifty species of water beetle have been recorded at Morton Lochs (Jackson 1964; Foster 1988) and the site is an important one for this group. Foster (1988) emphasised the relic nature of the Morton water beetles, concluding that the presence of several species of Haliplus and Gyrinus indicated survival of the original loch fauna.

At first this seems curious since Morton Lochs were only constructed in the first decade of this century. However, although most of Tentsmuir has been subject to drainage, some wet areas have persisted, and a hundred years ago small pools were created for grouse management (Berry 1894). Reference to Ainslie's map of 1785 (see Chapter 2) clearly shows Morton Lochs were not only present but larger at that time, though they are missing from a mid-nineteenth century map where only a drainage channel appears. The lochs are indicated on Roy's Military Survey of Scotland 1747–55, but it may be they have a pedigree going back to mesolithic times when the area formed a marshy slack flooded by the sea (Cole 1971).

b) Bugs – Hemiptera

Leaf hoppers – Homoptera

About 45 species were recorded from Tentsmuir Point NNR between 1963 and 1967 (Smith, 1971a).

Table 3.1: Invertebrate species recorded from Tentsmuir with Red Data Book, Notable or Habitat Indicator Status

a) Coleoptera – Beetles

i) Red Data Book, Category 3 – Rare

Arena tabida	Staphylinidae	TF	
Pissodes validirostris	Curculionidae	PW1	E

ii) Nationally notable species (A) less than 30 x 10 km sq.

Leiodes cinnamomea	Leiodidae		E
Magdalis duplicata	Curculionidae	PW1	E
Xantholinus tricolor	Staphylinidae		TP
Tropiphorus obtusus	Curculionidae		E
Cymnetron beccabungae	Curculionidae		ML

iii) Nationally notable species (B) known from less than 100 x 10 km sq.

Hydnobius perrisi	Leiodidae	TP
Acidota cruentata	Staphylinidae	TP
Aegialis sabuleti	Scarabaeidae	TP
Carabus nitens	Carabidae	TP
Cleonus piger	Curculionidae	E
Gyrinus caspius	Gyrinidae	TP
Hydnobius punctatus	Leiodidae	TP
Orthocerus clavicornis	Colydiidae	TP
Philonthus rotundicollis	Staphylinidae	TP
Rhantus frontalis	Dytiscidae	ML
Xantholinus laevigatus	Staphylinidae	TP
Atomaria strandi	Cryptophagidae	TP
Agabus labiotus	Dytiscisae	ML
Litodactylus leucogaster	Curculionidae	ML

iv) Rare or local in Scotland (C)

Morychus aeneus	Byrrhidae	E
Hister impressus	Histeridae	E
Baeckmanniolus dimidiatus	Histeridae	E
Acrotrichis insularis	Ptiliidae	TP
Aleochara moerens	Staphylinidae	TP
Olophrum fuscum	Staphylinidae	TP
Stenus geniculatus	Staphylinidae	TP
Dropophylla grandiloqua	Staphylinidae	TP

v) Fairly rare or local (D)

Chrysolina polita	Chrysomelidae		TP
Chrysolina hyperici	Chrysomelidae		TP
Magdalis phlegmatica	Curculionidae	PW2	E
Anthobium atrocephalum	Staphylinidae		TP
Melanimon tibiale	Tenebrionidae		TP
Omalium caesium	Staphylinidae		TP
Omalium rugulipenne	Staphylinidae		TP
Proteinus ovalis	Staphylinidae		TP

b) Hemiptera – Bugs

i) Nationally notable species (B) known from less than 100 x 10 km sq

Systellonotus triguttatus	Miridae	TP

ii) Rare or local in Scotland (C)

Ceratocombus coleoptratus	Dipsocoridae	TP
Coranus subapterus	Reduviidae	TP

c) Areneae – Spiders

i) Naturally notable species (B) known from less than 100 x 10 km sq
  Hyposinga albovittata   TP

ii) Rare or local in Scotland (C)
  Battyphantes parvulus   TP
  Widerra nodosa   TP

d) Diptera – True Flies

i) Red Data Book Category 3 – Rare
  Medetera pinicola   Dilichopodidae   TP

ii) Nationally notable species
  Goniopsita palposa   Chloropidae   TP
  Philonicus albiceps   Asilidae   TF

e) Lepidoptera

i) Nationally notable species (A)
Eupithecia trisionaria	Geometridae		TP
Paradiarsia sobrina	Noctuidae	D1	TP
Photedes elymi	Noctuidae	D1	TP

ii) Nationally notable species (B)
Agrostis ripae	Noctuidae	D1	TP
Eulamprotes wilkella	Gelechiidae		ML, TP
Euphitticia valerianatae	Geometridae		TP
Euxoa cursoria	Noctuidae	D1	TP
Noctua orbone	Noctuidae		TP, E
Ochropleura praeco	Noctuidae	D1	TP
Rhyacea simulans	Noctuidae		
Sideridis albicolon	Noctuidae	H3/D1	TP
Trifurculan griscella	Nepticulidae		TP
Phalomidia manniana	Cochylidae		ML

iii) Notable Scotland (C)
Somerinthus ocelleta	Sphinaidae		TP
Aethes smeathmanniana	Cochylidae		TP
Anerastrai lotella	Pyralidae		TP
Catarhoe cuculanta	Geometriade		TP
Phyllonorycter quinquegutella	Gracillanridae		TP
Chlio phragumitella	Pyralidae		ML

iv) Fairly local or rare (D)
  Perizoma affinantes   Cochylidae   ML

Abbreviations

PW1   Native Pinewood Indicator species
PW2   Pine species which occurs more widely than relic Caledonian forest
D1   Key Dune Indicator species
H3   Key Heath Indicator species
E   Recorded from Earlshall SSSI
ML   Recorded from Morton Lochs National Nature Reserve
TF   Recorded from Tentsmuir Forest
TP   Recorded from Tentsmuir Point National Nature Reserve

True bugs – Heteroptera

Collections were made at Tentsmuir Point NNR between 1963 and 1967 (Smith 1971b), in 1970 (Pelham-Clinton 1970) and in 1978 (Campbell 1980). Ninety species have been recorded of which the most notable is the Mirid bug (*Systellonotus triguttatus*) found in dune slacks where ants are common; the female is an ant mimic. Two other species known to have few stations in Scotland are given in Table 3.1b and include the predatory species *Coranus subapterus* – the aptly named Heath Assassin Bug.

c) Spiders – Aranae

A systematic survey of spiders of the Tentsmuir Point NNR was made in 1966 by members of the British Spider Study Group (Duffey 1968). Each habitat was worked until the number of new species recorded reached zero. A total of 143 species was recorded, approximately 23 percent of the total British spider fauna. Perhaps surprisingly almost all the species recorded were common, with three exceptions (Table 3.1c).

d) True Flies – Diptera

Although relatively few species have been collected, Tentsmuir is likely to be an important site for this group which makes up more than a fifth of the recorded invertebrates in Britain. If Tentsmuir held a tenth of these, approximately 600 species might be expected to occur.

A RDB Category 3 (Rare) species, *Medetera pinicola* was recently reported from pine logs on the Tentsmuir Point NNR (Rothery & Shaw 1989) and two other notable species have been reported Table 3.1d.

e) Moths – Lepidoptera

Surveys of the moths at Morton Lochs, Tentsmuir Point and Earlshall (Pelham-Clinton 1970; Skinner 1985; Clayton 1990, 1991; Welch 1989) have been carried out. About 270 species, around 11 percent of the British total, have been recorded of which about 20 are nationally notable species, are rare in Scotland or have only local distribution (Table 3.1e).

f) Other groups

The ITE survey, additionally, targeted millipedes (Diplopoda), woodlice (Isopods), and slugs and snails (Mollusca), but little comprehensive information is available for these or other groups. Liston (1980) has published a note on sawflies associated with creeping willow (*Salix repens*).

There is by comparison a wealth of information on butterflies and dragonflies, although both these groups are relatively poor in species. Both groups have high intrinsic public appeal, though none can be considered nationally rare or scarce in a Scottish context. Nevertheless, Tentsmuir holds important local concentrations of the following butterflies: Small Copper (*Lycaena phlaeas*), Small Heath (*Coenonympha pamphilus*), Common Blue (*Polyommatus icarus*), Ringlet (*Aphantopus hyperantus*), Dark-green Fritillary (*Argynnis aglaga*), Small pearl-bordered Fritillary (*Boloria selene*), Green Hairstreak (*Callophrys rubi*) and is the only extant Fife locality for Grayling (*Hipparchia semele*) (Smout & Kinnear 1993a).

All the common Fife dragonfly and damselfly species breed at Tentsmuir, including two recent colonists: the Azure Damselfly (*Coenagrion puella*) and the Common Darter (*Sympetrum striolatum*) (Smout & Kinnear 1993b, Kinnear *pers obs*).

Statutory Protection

In the small parts of Tentsmuir that have been studied, about 1500 species of invertebrate have been recorded, although the two most abundant taxa in species number are seriously under-represented: flies (Diptera) and bees, wasps and allies (Hymenoptera). It is likely that up to 3000 species of invertebrate live somewhere on Tentsmuir, i.e. about a tenth of those found in the whole of Britain. The known invertebrate interest, together with information on the plant, physiographic and bird interests have formed the basis for parts of Tentsmuir receiving their statutory protection.

Nature conservation as a form of land use is still a relatively new feature. The first formally designated nature reserves in Britain only came into being after the 1949 National Parks and Access to the Countryside Act. Morton Lochs was made a NNR in 1952, only the second to be declared in Scotland after Beinn Eighe. Tentsmuir Point was made an NNR in 1954. There have been extensions to both sites including Tayport Heath, which is leased from Forest Enterprise.

SSSI designation extends to Earlshall Muir, St Michael's Wood, the Eden Estuary and Tayport Bay. The total area now enjoying statutory protection is approximately 2700 ha. (see Fig. 1 and Appendix 2). However much of this is tidal and irrelevant to the interests of terrestrial invertebrates. Moreover site designation was originally seen as giving protection to a representative national series of key habitats at a time when both agriculture and forestry practices were less intensive and less damaging to wildlife. Little knowledge was available to determine whether any designated areas were large enough to support viable populations of any key species or communities.

Many British invertebrates are in serious decline and their needs are not always being met even on sites designated as nature reserves.

General Characteristics of Invertebrate Ecological Requirements

Invertebrates are, in general, much more sensitive to habitat change than are most plants or vertebrates. Why is this and what are the characteristics that make invertebrates vulnerable?

a) Most have annual life cycles, often with two or more generations a year. Suitable conditions must be present every year. Many species have complex life histories and many have different habitat requirements at each different stage. Obvious examples are most butterflies and flying insects which have aquatic larvae stages such as dragonflies.

b) Many invertebrates exploit only precise components of their habitat, often being restricted to one host plant species or a particular part of a plant. They therefore have very precise habitat requirements and are often consequently rare.

c) Most invertebrates are small and inhabit micro habitats which are often trivial features of any site but which may be vital at some stage in their life cycle. These features can easily be overlooked by land managers interested in nature conservation.

d) Many species are sedentary and have limited powers of dispersal.

e) Although invertebrates may pass the hottest or coldest part of the year in a temporary resting stage, they must complete their life cycle to survive. This is unlike plants, the seeds of which may remain in the soil for many years and only germinate when suitable conditions occur.

Looking at some examples from Tentsmuir, Duffey (1968) found that in general most spider species were found in several dune habitats but their numbers tended to peak in only one habitat. Although 21 species of spider were found on the strandline, only one of these (*Filoneropus ambiguis*) was not found anywhere else. Clearly the strandline is not the most hospitable habitat in which to live permanently and most of the species found in summer on the strandline, foredunes and yellow dunes were found to migrate inland in the autumn. Immature stages of some dune spiders appear to have habitat preferences different from their adults. Over half the species of spider recorded at Tentsmuir were found in dune slacks, reflecting the high degree of structural diversity found there. Spider species which occurred widely inland tended to show a marked preference for certain habitats in the dunes.

Amongst the Lepidoptera, the White Colon (*Sideridis albicolon*) and Grayling butterfly (*Hipparchia semele*) are good examples of species which are found on inland heaths or unimproved grassland further south in Britain, but tend to become confined to the coastal zone in higher latitudes, although neither is exclusively associated with dunes. However, the Sand Dart (*Agrostis ripae*) is both limited to the coast and exclusive to sand dunes throughout its British range. Moreover it tends to keep to the very outer dune zone and its larvae often feed on Sea Rocket (*Cakile maritima*), an annual plant which grows only along the strandline. Another moth restricted to the active foredunes is the Lyme Grass (*Photedes elymi*), the larvae of which, as might be suggested by its common name, is restricted to a single host plant of the same name *Leymus arenarius*.

Sand Dune Habitats and their Management for Invertebrates

Since the habitat requirements of each individual species may be very precise, how can management for their conservation be set about without knowledge of these requirements? It is quite clear that with the number of species involved, it will never be possible to amass a full knowledge of their ecology. However, owing to the experience gained by specialists in a variety of conservation and research organisations, guidelines are now available to take account of habitat features which are vital for invertebrates, but vulnerable, without necessarily knowing which species are present (Kirby 1992).

1. Shingle

Shingle is a less hostile environment for invertebrates than for plants. The richest invertebrate fauna occur on stable shingle with some established vegetation. The communities which shingle supports are very slow to establish and are maintained by natural forces of wave and wind action. Consequently the best management advice for invertebrate conservation is to leave it alone. Lucky Scalp, within the Tayport-Tentsmuir Coast SSSI, is the only shingle feature which extends above the high water mark at present, though it has yet to be examined for its invertebrates.

2. Saltmarsh

All levels of saltmarsh support interesting invertebrate communities, but the richest tend to be where they grade into freshwater or terrestrial habitats. This is often the location for stands of Sea Club-rush (*Bolboschoenus maritimus*) or reed (*Phragmites australis*) which provide over-wintering sites for species which spend the summer on the saltmarsh. The largest saltmarshes at Tentsmuir are in Tayport Bay and the Eden Estuary, but these are small even by Scottish standards. Temporary saltmarsh communities of Sea-blite (*Suaeda maritima*) and Glasswort (*Salicornia europaea*) occur in the tidal lagoon at Tentsmuir Point. Saltmarshes which have not been managed tend to be best for invertebrates and the deliberate introduction of stock grazing is not advised. The saltmarsh in Tayport Bay is subject to locally moderate rabbit grazing.

3. Strandline and Upper Foreshore

The upper shore plants tend to host communities of specialist invertebrates. Accumulations of seaweed provide breeding sites for many beetles and flies. Often the most numerous invertebrates are burrowing amphipod crustacea – the sand hoppers. Beach cleaning in any form – collection of drift wood for barbecues or wholesale removal of rotting material by beach cleaning machines for public amenity – is the greatest hazard for these communities. At present all the Tentsmuir beaches are free from any form of regular beach management.

4. Dunes and Slacks

Large dune systems like Tentsmuir which exhibit a full range of habitats from mobile foredune, through dense marram yellow dunes and fixed grey dunes to sandy heathland with intermediate dune slacks, are best for invertebrates. Structural diversity of vegetation is important, as are the gaps between tussock-dominated areas. However the importance of areas of bare ground needs to be stressed. On Tentsmuir and on many other sand dune areas in Britain and Western Europe, loss of bare sand has adversely affected many invertebrates which use it for basking, hunting, burrowing, resting or incubating their eggs.

The invertebrate fauna in dune slacks include specialists found in no other wetland habitat. The most valuable slacks are those that flood each winter but dry out in the summer. At Tentsmuir the dune system has been much modified by extensive drainage and rechanneling of natural water courses. Winter flooding of slacks does not occur every year and is a major factor in influencing the direction of habitat change. On Tentsmuir Point NNR, in recent years, many of the slacks have been invaded by scrub, mostly Common Sallow (*Salix atrocinerea*) and Silver Birch (*Betula*

pendula). The development of some taller scrub and woodland can encourage interesting invertebrate communities and this habitat is well represented on Earlshall
Muir. However, such development should not be at the expense of previously more
open habitats on which the typical coastal invertebrates depend.

Most dune systems including Tentsmuir have been traditionally grazed for long
periods in the past (Doody 1985; Kirby 1992; Chapter 2 above). Part of Tentsmuir,
Earlshall Muir, has been continuously grazed right up to the present by sheep and
cattle. Identification of the levels of stock grazing appropriate to the survival of the
vegetation and invertebrate communities is difficult (Doody 1985; Leach 1985).
Grazing by domestic stock and rabbits may produce a close vegetation sward which
is floristically rich but poor in invertebrate communities. Grazing should be sufficient to maintain a varied vegetation structure (Kirby 1992).

Invertebrate Distribution Patterns

Other important Tentsmuir semi-natural habitats such as fens, heathland, acid grassland, deciduous woodland or freshwater will not be dealt with here. The distribution
of some butterfly species in Fife will be examined so as to illustrate the variation of
distribution patterns that are likely to be typical for many other invertebrates. Note
that the example provisional distribution maps should be compared with the effort
map (Fig. 3.1a). The maps show distributions recorded within 1 km squares.

Example 1: Small Tortoiseshell (Fig. 3.1b)

Characteristic of a widespread and common species, with wide ecological tolerance.
The larval foodplants tend to be common weed species which are also widely dis-
tributed. The species may be wholly mobile and is not tied to any particular habitat
type. The recorded distribution is largely a reflection of effort and gaps in distribution are likely to be entirely due to under-recording.

The example is one of Fife's most familiar butterflies the Small Tortoiseshell
(*Aglais urticae*). Other species which may be expected to show a similar pattern of
occurrence with sufficient recording effort are: Green-veined White (*Pieris napi*),
Small White (*P. rapae*), Large White (*P. brassicae*), Red Admiral (*Vanessa ata-
lanta*) and Painted Lady (*Cynthia cardui*). The latter two species are continental mi-
grants which occasionally breed here, but typically roam widely. The Large and
Small White are notable pests on brassica crops, but can also utilise wildflower host
plants, and neither is territorial.

Small tortoiseshell larvae feed on the common nettle (*Urtica dioica*) while the
Green-veined White has several host plants which are extremely common. They are
the earliest-flying butterflies and tolerant of lower temperatures than other species
and, excluding Shetland, occur throughout Scotland.

Example 2: Ringlet (Fig. 3.1c)

This shows a common species with a distribution limited to the north of Fife. In
other parts of Britain such range restrictions might reflect the underlying geology,
since some invertebrates exclusively feed on lime loving-plants which are confined

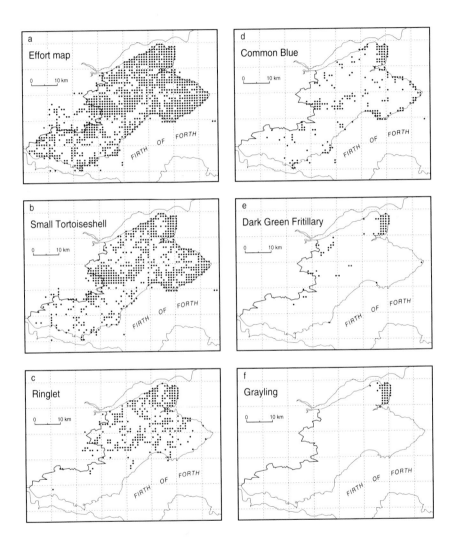

Figure 3.1 (a–f): Distribution patterns of butterflies in Fife

to base-rich soils, or it might indicate the geographical limit of range of a specific host plant.

This example is the Ringlet and the limiting ecological factor is most likely related to air pollution. As mentioned earlier, insects can respond rapidly to environmental changes. The pattern of Ringlet distribution in Fife has altered markedly since the last national survey in the 1970s (Heath *et al.* 1984). Ringlets are currently extending their range southwards in Fife at rate of approximately 1 km per year and there is a similar expansion in other parts of central Scotland. This may indicate that certain types of air pollution are decreasing as heavy polluting industries have declined.

Example 3: Common Blue (Fig. 3.1d)

Although the records show a widespread distribution it is distinctly patchy. Records tend to be concentrated on the Lomond Hills, Lochore/Benarty, the Cults ridge, the coastal fringe and, of course, Tentsmuir. All are areas where there are relatively large tracts of remaining semi-natural vegetation. This suggests that this species has narrower ecological requirements than the last two examples.

The Common Blue is largely restricted to unimproved grasslands, heaths and ruderal communities. Such habitats, though still common, are much fragmented, tending to be replaced by improved grassland and conifer woodland at a relatively rapid rate (Tudor *et al.* 1994). In Fife, the Common Blue is associated almost entirely with the widespread Common Birdsfoot-trefoil (*Lotus corniculatus*), though this is only one of several larval food plants elsewhere. Common Blues do not thrive where sward heights exceed 15 cm, which restricts them to areas subject to some form of grazing regime or which are occasionally disturbed through some other man-made activity. Like many blue butterfly species they tend to have symbiotic relationships with ants. Small Copper and Small Heath show similar distributions, restricted to semi-natural open habitats even though their larval foodplants may be abundant and widespread. They can all survive in the agricultural landscape but only around the margins of cultivated land.

Example 4: Dark Green Fritillary (Fig. 3.1e)

This species clearly has a much more restricted range. Its ecological requirements are even more exacting. The habitat in which it can still survive in Fife is exceedingly rare. Although further recording is likely to yield many more locations in the west of Fife, these are likely to be of small populations vulnerable to development pressures or major habitat alteration.

This distribution is for Dark Green Fritillary, which can be seen in ones or twos at most of its Fife stations. It can only be regarded as common on Tentsmuir, though even here it is unusual to see three or four individuals together. The larvae feed exclusively on violets (*Viola* spp), but the species survives in a surprising variety of habitats. Small Pearl-bordered Fritillary and Green Hairstreak also show very restricted distributions, the former to wet heath/grassland, fens and damp areas in open woodland and the latter to heath with Bilberry (*Vaccinium myrtilis*). These species only survive on remnant semi-natural habitats and are very rarely encountered on cultivated land.

Example 5:Grayling (Fig. 3.1f)

The last example shows a species confined to a single locality, effectively genetically isolated from adjacent populations to the north and south. Since the area it occupies is still relatively large, it may be common and in some years even abundant when conditions are ideal, but it would be entirely vulnerable to any major land use change, such as conversion to arable use.

This example is the Grayling which is now found only on Tentsmuir, although it was known from other sites on the south coast of Fife in the last century. Most dune areas in Fife have been modified by agriculture, or used for housing development, forestry plantations, golf courses etc., which have tended to eliminate suitable habitat. As mentioned previously, the Grayling is not entirely a coastal species in the southern part of its range. On Tentsmuir it is absent from the western half of the dune system which has long been cultivated. It is common in the remaining open areas of Tentsmuir and rapidly re-colonises, albeit temporarily, clear felled areas of plantation. Although a strong flier and able to cope with the windswept conditions on Tentsmuir, the Eden estuary remains an effective barrier to apparently suitable habitat at Out Head and the St Andrews links. Other butterflies now restricted to one or two localities in Fife, but which were undoubtedly more widespread a century ago, are the Large Heath, threatened by further conifer afforestation, and the Northern Brown Argus, still vulnerable to small-scale, coastal developments.

Discussion

These different distribution patterns for Fife butterflies may well prove to be typical of many other invertebrates as further records accumulate. They can also be used to illustrate the sequence of range reduction that many invertebrate species are likely to have experienced as major landuse changes have occurred and semi-natural habitats have become smaller and fragmented.

Increased fragmentation of habitat means that many species effectively end up living on separate islands, some of which are not large enough or do not enjoy all the requirements to sustain viable populations. If an event occurs which causes a population to die out at any site, re-colonisation becomes less likely with increased distance to the neighbouring population.

It might be expected that flying insects like butterflies would have no trouble at all in re-occupying vacant sites, and this is undoubtedly true for most of our common species like the Small Tortoiseshell, Large and Small Whites, and is a characteristic of their behaviour which enables them to remain common. For the more specialised species, movement between adjacent colonies probably only occurs occasionally. For many flightless invertebrates with poor powers of dispersal, inter-habitat island movement does not occur, and small-scale local extinctions must be a common and unrecorded occurrence.

Fife is one of the most modified regions in Scotland. Improved grassland and arable make up 72 per cent of the area (Tudor *et al.* 1994). Housing, industry, roads, reservoirs, conifer plantations, parkland, quarries and recreational areas account for another 18 per cent. Semi-natural habitats tend to be small and very fragmented and make up less than 10 per cent of the land area. As a consequence, apart from some common species with wide ecological tolerances, the distribution of many invertebrate species in Fife will be similarly fragmented.

Conclusion

Many of the beetles, bugs, moths and other invertebrates which have been identified as being notable on Tentsmuir are likely to be found at only a handful of sites within Fife region. Further losses of remaining semi-natural areas elsewhere in Fife will tend to heighten Tentsmuir's importance as a refuge from extinction.

Current and future managers of the Tentsmuir area, be they farmers, foresters, from local authorities or government agencies, all have a vital part to play which will determine which species will survive to bite, amuse and delight our grandchildren.

Bibliography

Balfour, J H, *Excursions to Tentsmuir* (Notes from the Royal Botanic Gardens, 1902), vol. 2

Ball, S G, *Invertebrates Site Register,* No. 66. Terrrestrial and Freshwater Invertebrates with Red Data Book, Notable or Habitat Indicator Status (unpublished Nature Conservancy Council Report, 1986)

Berry, W, 'On the introduction of grouse to the Tentsmuir in Fife', *Annals of Scottish Natural History*, 12 (1894), pp. 197–203

Campbell, J K, 'The true bugs (Heteroptera) of Tentsmuir Point, Fife', *Forth Naturalist and Historian* (1980), pp. 72–85

Clayton, J, 'Lepidoptera Survey, Morton Lochs NNR' (unpublished report to Nature Conservancy Council, 1990)

Clayton, J, 'Interesting Lepidoptera records from North-East Fife', *Entomologist's Monthly Magazine,* 103 (1991), pp. 297–9

Coles, J M, 'The Early Settlement of Scotland: Excavations at Morton, Fife', *Proceedings of the Prehistoric Society,* XXXVII (1971), p. 287

Cotton, M J, 'Fauna', *Dundee and District,* ed. Jones, S J (British Association for Advancement Science, 1968), pp. 82–93

Cotton, M J, 'The distribution of *Boreus hymalis* (L.) (Mecoptera) on a sand dune system', *Entomologist's Monthly Magazine,* 106 (1971), pp. 174–6

Cotton, M J and Miller, P F, 'A population of *Cylindroiulus latestriatus* (Curtis) on sand dunes', *Symposia of the Zoological Society of London*, 32 (1974), pp. 589–602

Crapper, E, 'A first list of the flowering plants and ferns of Tentsmuir, Fife' (ms. Library Botany Dept., University of St Andrews, 1940)

Crapper, E, 'A first list of the plants of Tentsmuir Nature Reserve' (ms. list SNH files, Cupar, 1956)

Crapper, E, 'Corrections and additions to 1956 list' (ms. list SNH files, Cupar, 1957)

Crawford, R M M and Wishart, D, 'A multivariate analysis of the development of dune slack variation in relation to coastal accretion at Tentsmuir, Fife', *Journal of Ecology,* 54 (1966), pp. 729–43

Deshmukh, I K, 'Primary production and leaf litter breakdown of *Ammophila arenaria* in a sand dune succession' (Ph.D. thesis, University of Dundee, 1974)

Dodd, C, 'A report on the beetles on Tentsmuir NNR summer 1978' (unpublished report to the Nature Conservancy Council, 1978)

Doody, J P, 'The conservation of sand dunes in Great Britain – a review', *Sand dunes and their Management. Focus on Nataure Conservation,* ed. Doody, J P (Nature Conservancy Council, 1985), no. 13, pp. 43–56

Duffey, E, 'An ecological analysis of the spider fauna of sand dunes', *Journal of Animal*

Ecology, 37 (1968), pp. 641–74

Foster, G N, 'Water beetles of the Morton Lochs and Loch Fitty, Fife' (unpublished report to the Nature Conservancy Council, 1988)

Gimingham, C H, 'Maritime and sub-maritime communities', *The Vegetation of Scotland,* ed. Burnett, J H (Oliver & Boyd, 1964)

Howie, C, 'Flora of Fife and Kinross' (ms. Library of Botany Dept., University of St Andrews, 1884)

Ingram, H, 'Vegetation and flora', *Dundee and District,* ed. Jones, S J (British Association for the Advancement of Science, 1968)

Jackson, D J, 'Water beetles collected in the Morton Lochs Nature Reserve, Fife', *Scottish Naturalist,* 71 (1964), pp. 95–7.

Kirby, P, *Habitat Management for Invertebrates: a practical handbook* (Royal Society for the Protection of Birds, 1992)

Leach, S J, 'The problem of setting grazing levels on dune heath, Earlshall Muir, Fife', *Sand dunes and their management. Focus on Nature Conservation,* ed. Doody, J P (Nature Conservancy Council, 1985), no. 13, pp. 135–43

Liston, A, 'Notes on sawflies (Hym., Symphyta) collected in Scotland', *Entomologist's Monthly Magazine,* 115 (1980), pp. 239–43

Pelham-Clinton, E J, 'Lepidoptera collected in Tentsmuir NNR' (unpublished list, SNH files, Cupar, 1970)

Poore, M E D, 'Plants on Tentsmuir' (unpublished list, SNH files, Cupar, 1954)

Robertson, D R, 'Notes on Tentsmuir, Fifeshire' (ms. Library Dept. of Botany, St Andrews University, 1915)

Rotheray, G E and Shaw, M R, 'Medetera cocoons under bark (Dipt. Dilichopodidae)', *Entomologist's Monthly Magazine* (1989), pp. 125, 174

Shaw, R, 'Tentsmuir and its flora', *Journal of the Forestry Commission,* 14 (1935), pp. 107–10

Skinner, B, 'Lepidoptera noted from Tentsmuir NNR 9–13 August 1985' (unpublished list, SNH Files, Cupar, 1985)

Smith, M, 'A provisional list of Coleoptera from Tentsmuir Point NNR 1963–67' (unpublished report to the Nature Conservancy Council, 1971a)

Smith, M, 'A summary of recent and unlisted additions to the flora and fauna of the reserve' (unpublished report to Nature Conservancy Council, 1971b)

Smith, W G, 'Botanical survey of Scotland: Forfar and Fife', *Scottish Geographical Magazine,* 21 (1905), pp. 57–83

Smout, A-M and Kinnear, P K, *The Butterflies of Fife: A Provisional Atlas* (Fife Regional Council, 1993a), p. 29

Smout, A-M and Kinnear, P K, *The Dragonflies of Fife: A Provisional Atlas* (Fife Regional Council, 1993b), p. 17

Tudor, G J, Mackey, E C and Underwood, F M, *The National Countryside Monitoring Scheme* (Main Report, Scottish Natural Heritage, 1994)

Welch, R C, '*Orthcerus clavicornis* (L.) (Col. Colydiidae) *Melanimon tibiale* (F.) (Col. Tenebrionidae) and *Notoxus monocerus* (L.) (Col. Anthicidae) from coastal dunes in Scotland', *Entomologist's Monthly Magazine,* 114 (1979), pp. 249–50

Welch, R C, 'Invertebrates of Scottish Sand Dunes', *Proceedings of the Royal Society of Edinburgh,* 96B (1989), pp. 267–87

West, G, 'Flora of Scottish Lakes', *Proceedings of the Royal Society of Edinburgh* (1910), pp. 151–2

4

The Birds of Tentsmuir, 1880–1990: An Ecological Catastrophe?

Anne-Marie Smout

There is probably no finer stretch of seaside moorland in Scotland than that which extends from the estuary of the Eden to the estuary of the Tay... (Wilson 1910)

Introduction

This chapter is based on data gathered from published and unpublished sources, mainly from amateur naturalists, during the last hundred years, rather than on any rigorous personal field research, although I have visited Tentsmuir on innumerable occasions and made observations as an amateur birdwatcher during the last 10–15 years, and latterly as Recorder for Fife Nature, Fife's Biological Records Centre. The chapter describes some of the environmental changes which have taken place, looks at the effect on the bird population, and ends with a brief comparison of what has happened at the Ythan estuary, a very similar area north of Aberdeen.

Tentsmuir has changed more within living memory than probably at any other time during its entire history and the effect on the bird population has been equally drastic, especially on the breeding population. No attention is given here to the Eden estuary, bordering on Tentsmuir to the south, which has an ecosystem all of its own, although the shore round to Shelly Point, south east of Leuchars Airfield, is included. The estuary supports large numbers of wintering birds, but even here few duck, waders or terns now manage to breed successfully.

Tentsmuir was, not so long ago, considered to be of national importance for birds and one of the prime breeding sites in Scotland for a number of species. It was to become the first real nature reserve in Scotland, when Fife County Council adopted The Wild Bird Protection Act (1894) for the area in 1896. This is discussed in some detail by J A Harvie-Brown, Scotland's foremost ornithologist at the turn of the century and editor and author of a series of 'Vertebrate Faunas', covering the whole of Scotland. In the volume *A Fauna of the Tay Basin and Strathmore,* he wrote enthusiastically about 'the great wealth of bird-life' here, and the importance of 'careful preservation of defined tracts of famous breeding quarters of colonies of our birds like those of Tents Muir.' (Harvie-Brown 1906.) When Miss Baxter and Miss Rintoul published *The Birds of Scotland* in 1953 they could still write 'Between the mouth of the Eden and Tay is a long stretch of sand, inshore from which lies the expanse of sand-hills known as Tentsmuir, a famous bird sanctuary and nesting place', though things were already changing then, because they added, 'A good deal of Tentsmuir, however, has now been planted up by the Forestry Commission' (Baxter

& Rintoul 1953). *A Check-list of the Birds of Tentsmuir* (Grierson 1962) appeared as a special supplement to *Scottish Birds,* the newly launched journal of the Scottish Ornithologists' Club. Grierson was the secretary of the Dundee branch of the SOC and spent a lot of time at Tentsmuir during the 1950s. His very full and excellent account states that 'Tentsmuir, which forms the north-east corner of Fife, has generally been looked upon as of some importance in the overall picture of birds in Scotland' (Grierson 1962). Another very detailed account of the habitat and birds of Tentsmuir is contained in Henry Boase's unpublished manuscript *The Birds of North Fife* (1964) and produced for private circulation. Boase's work is based largely on personal observations over several decades and has a whole chapter on 'The changing face of Tentsmuir'. Today, no ornithologist could write so lyrically about Tentsmuir let alone include it in a list of nationally important sites, so what has happened?

An early description of Tentsmuir can be found in *The Statistical Account of Scotland*, under the parish of Leuchars. There is no mention of birds, but under the neighbouring parish of Ferry-Port-on-Craig (now Tayport), is recorded:

> Several kinds of sea fowls frequent the shore during winter. Every year, about the month of April, they leave the coast, to go and hatch their young. They return again in the month of August, when they take their annual flight. They are immediately succeeded by other sea fowls, that make their appearance here in the spring, remain during the summer months and hatch about the shore. In the month of August or September, they remove from this to their winter habitation. Thus they follow each other in constant succession every year. (Dalgleish 1796.)

It was not till the following century that more detailed accounts of the birds began to appear. John Guille Millais, Victorian sportsman *par excellence,* bird artist and author of a series of books on birds and wildfowling in Scotland, considered Tentsmuir to be 'the foremost Teal resort in the country', though a fresh attempt to drain the muir in 1876 had 'greatly reduced the population of Teal' (Millais 1902).

The most evocative description of what Tentsmuir used to be like, however, was given by William Berry of Tayfield who in 1894 wrote:

> The Tents Muir is a large tract of barren moorland, flat as the sea which borders it along its entire length... The elevation above sea-level of the whole of this area is quite inconsiderable – perhaps eight or ten feet, or even less; but it is broken up and partially sheltered from the sweep of the winds by lines or chains of sandhills, which rise to the height of thirty or forty feet, and trend, speaking generally, in the direction from east to west; a similar chain forms a continuous rampart along the seashore.

He knew the place intimately because he leased the sporting rights of the most northerly section from 1890 and was to control it until 1919, when the estate was acquired by Dundee Town Council. What is known about the birds of Tentsmuir during this period is largely due to Berry, and Harvie-Brown recorded his great debt to W Berry's knowledge of the status of species on Tentsmuir in *A Fauna of the Tay Basin and Strathmore.* Tentsmuir was then divided into three parts: Earlshall Muir in the south, Kinshaldy Muir in the middle, and Shanwell Muir – also called 'Scotscraig' – to the north. It was Scotscraig which W Berry leased, and all his notes and correspondence therefore relate to this area, although there is no reason to believe that the other two sections differed greatly from Scotscraig. W Berry's description continues:

> The soil, if such it can be called, is simply blown sand, only anchored in its present position by the vegetation which has somehow established itself upon the surface... a strong gale sometimes makes a material alteration in the appearance and size of the sandhills, blowing tons of sand, along with the bent grass – root and stem – which formerly bound it together, to form a new and sterile area on what was before good heather ground...

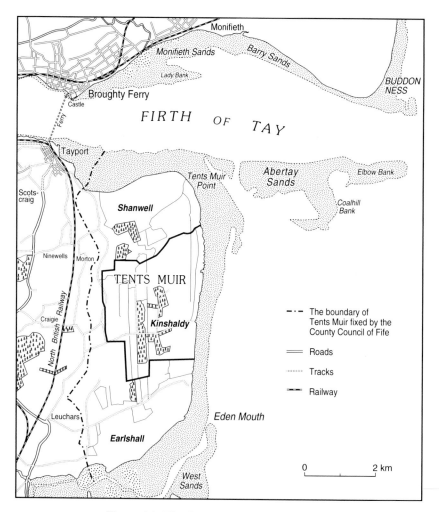

Figure 4.1: The three divisions of Tentsmuir
(after Harvie-Brown 1906)

It was a combination of factors which made Tentsmuir so attractive to birds: its remoteness meant that disturbance from human activities was generally low; the moorland had few trees, leaving the land very open, which gave birds the chance of seeing predators a long way off; and perhaps most important of all, water was abundant with lots of little pools everywhere. When the legendary eruption of Pallas's Sand-Grouse took place in 1888 – with 1500–2000 birds visiting Scotland – the largest numbers in Fife were found at Tentsmuir, with up to 200 birds being reported from the heather moor (W Berry, unpublished notes). The moors were, however, especially important for breeding birds: large numbers of Eider, Shelduck, Teal, Shoveler, Dunlin, Golden Plover, Black and Red grouse and Corncrake nested regularly, while Redshank and Snipe were considered positively common breeders. Red Grouse had been successfully introduced by a previous owner in 1876 to boost the small local population and they flourished up to World War One, with 40–60 brace shot annually (Smith 1948). This followed a system where Berry artificially increased the waterholes on Scotscraig Muir by blocking all drains and ditches, so that quite large areas flooded, and it was here that Dunlin bred (J Berry, *pers. comm.*). Harvie-Brown (1906) reported 'a great and charming increase in the wild things' following the adoption of the Wild Birds Act and vigorous protection to keep predation by crows, foxes and weasels in check, and stopping illegal shooting of birds and wholesale egg collecting. Organised egg collectors had been in the habit of sailing across from Dundee to raid any nests they could find, and the Eiders and the many terns breeding on or near the shore were particularly easy targets. Common Terns were then considered the most abundant tern species, but Arctic Terns and Sandwich Terns nested, as well as 'some twenty pairs' of Little Terns nesting in 1886–88, increasing to 'some thirty pairs' in 1904. Millais had at one time received reports of Roseate Terns 'among the large colony which breeds along the coast from the Icehouse as far as the Eden mouth', but two days of searching had failed to detect anything but the common species (Harvie-Brown 1906).

All of this came an to end with the outbreak of World War One. Protection largely ceased, and egg collecting and other predation once more took its toll. More seriously, the entire face of Tentsmuir was to change dramatically when most of the area was given over to forestry plantations after the end of the war. The three sections of Tentsmuir suffered different fates.

Although Scotscraig Muir was acquired by Dundee Town Council, W Berry had been keen to buy it as there were rumours that it would make a good site for industry and a ship building company showed interest (J Berry, *pers. comm.*) but nothing happened until the eventual sale to the Forestry Commission. Berry (1939), Boase (1964) and Grierson (1962) all describe how planting was started immediately and the moor enclosed with wire-netting to keep rabbits out and protect the young trees. However, the wire fencing was of too small a mesh to allow the ducklings to pass through and reach the sea from the nest sites among the newly-planted trees. When the forestry workers saw what was happening, they did their best to lift stranded ducklings across the fences, but very many perished each year until eventually the trees grew too big and birds stopped breeding here. Only the terns continued to breed on the sand at Scotscraig but egg collectors and other predators meant that each year, they lost most of their eggs and eventually they also left the area for good.

Kinshaldy Muir had already been acquired by the Forestry Commission in 1921 and planted with conifers with similar effects to those on Scotscraig Muir. According to J P F Keddie of Tayport, who knew the area well as a boy, this section had also been looked after for many years to preserve the bird life and, as on the Scotscraig section, birds of the moorland and the shore could be seen in vast numbers at nesting time (Keddie, unpublished note). There are no early data for this area.

Only Earlshall Muir was actively protected by the owner, although a considerable area to the south-west had to be sold to the RAF for airfield construction at the time of World War One. The rest was still largely unchanged and many birds now moved to Earlshall, so much so that by 1936 breeding numbers here became comparable with those on the former sites (Grierson 1962). The extension of RAF Leuchars in 1942, however, and the use of the whole of Tentsmuir as a military training ground (it had already been used as an artillery range in the 1930s) had a drastic effect on the bird life. A further loss of muir took place when the Forestry Commission acquired about a third of Earlshall to plant what is now known as Reres Wood, near the airfield. During the war, egg collecting as well as trapping and shooting adult birds for food once again became a serious hazard for breeding birds, and this practice apparently went unchecked for some years after the war (Grierson 1962; Boase 1964).

National and economic events had thus over-ruled the importance of Tentsmuir as a bird sanctuary, but it was far from the case that its importance for wildlife had been forgotten. A number of people were fully aware of what was happening and deeply regretted the loss of this unique habitat. After World War Two, therefore, serious endeavours were made to preserve at least some of Tentsmuir in its original form and so the remotest part of Tentsmuir Point emerged as a National Nature Reserve in 1954.

Another important location for birds in the Tentsmuir area were the Morton Lochs. These two lochs occupied open, hummocky ground with only the odd tree providing a little shelter, and were, in the 1890s, stocked with young carp imported from Italy. Some years later it was found that Swan mussels (*Anadonta cygnea*) had become established in the lochs, imported as embryos attached to the introduced fish (J Berry *pers. comm.*). These mussels attracted ducks which visited the lochs in great numbers, and because the lochs were situated so close to the sea, sea duck and even divers found their way there. Boase (1964) lists 109 species recorded at Morton Lochs, among them Black-throated Diver and Red-throated Diver, Whooper Swan, Bewick's Swan and Mute Swan, Eider, Shelduck, Scaup, Common Scoter, Velvet Scoter and Long-tailed Duck. A pair of Common Scoter also bred at Tentsmuir on at least one occasion (1947). The shallow lochs were outstanding for waders: Redshank, Dunlin, Golden Plover, Snipe, Curlew and Lapwing nested close by, with records of visiting rarities such as Bittern, Great Snipe and Buff-breasted Sandpiper, and also Jack Snipe, Grey Plover, Whimbrel, Black-tailed Godwit, Bar-tailed Godwit, Wood Sandpiper, Green Sandpiper, Spotted Redshank, Greenshank, Little Stint, Ringed Plover, Curlew, Sandpiper and Ruff, as well as many other interesting birds: all five species of grebe, Garganey, Gadwall, Wigeon, Red-crested Pochard, Red-breasted Merganser, Goosander, Black Tern, Wheatear, Whinchat, Stonechat and Kingfisher. The list is extraordinary to the eyes of present-day ornithologists.

Scottish Natural Heritage now manage both Tentsmuir Point and Morton Lochs for their wildlife interests, but things have not always been easy. Two major problems have been an increasing shortage of water and the encroachment of trees. The many trees planted on very sandy soil diminished the groundwater, and constant and more efficient ways of draining the surrounding farmland in the last 40 years have lowered the water table by four feet. Dispute over the water supply to Morton Lochs arose in the 1980s, after the burn which fed the lochs had been diverted some time during the 1970s by the local farmer, apparently without any objection from the Nature Conservancy Council. The lochs began to dry out for much longer periods and rank vegetation started to invade, so that visitors were as likely to see roe deer as ducks or waders from the hides put up by the NCC. Substantial work involving large machinery was carried out to deepen the lochs, but lack of water remained a problem. However, in 1993 an agreement was reached between SNH and the local farmer to redirect the flow of the burn back through the lochs, allowing the farmer to take water from the burn when necessary. This has already been beneficial to the water level, though it is too early to say if it will be sufficient to bring back the birds. It has also been suggested that encroachment by too many tall trees around the lochs is now making the lochs less attractive to ducks and waders.

Earlshall was for many years managed and protected by the owner for wildlife. In the 1980s, however, the muir was sold and SNH now compensate the new owners for foregone income to keep the area undeveloped, although with the general lowering of the water table even Earlshall Muir has become much drier.

An impressive list of 192 species for the whole of Tentsmuir was given by Grierson (1962), with 65 species regarded as regular breeders. They included Teal, Shoveler, Tufted Duck, Eider, Shelduck, Ringed Plover, Snipe, Redshank, Sandwich, Common, Arctic and Little Terns, as well as a number of small birds such as Wheatears, Stonechats, Spotted Flycatcher and various warblers.

Grierson stated that 'as a nesting place of terns, Tentsmuir was until 1924 one of the most important on the east coast, probably second only to the Farne Islands off Northumberland' (1962). As already mentioned, the main breeding area was at that time Scotscraig, but as the forestry plantation matured many birds moved south to Earlshall, which during the 1950–60s sustained numbers comparable to those which had been present at Scotscraig. The greatest disturbance was now from low-flying jet aircraft and other activities from the nearby airfield (which on more than one occasion caused whole colonies to desert their nests), egg collectors and holiday makers, as well as the foxes and crows which found excellent shelter among the trees. Grierson advocated some form of protection to help the tern populations to return to something like their former strength. Protection was certainly afforded by gamekeepers on Earlshall while a great deal of effort was put in by private individuals in the 1950s to help guard the nest sites on the shore, and when the International Union for the Conservation of Nature and Natural Resources met in Edinburgh in 1956, the delegates could be shown five species of tern breeding on Tentsmuir (J Berry *pers. comm.*).

It is often difficult to compare modern data with historical accounts because relative statements such as 'many' or 'exceptional numbers' were used frequently rather than actual counts. Thus W Berry commented that the Common Tern 'has bred on the moor all my life in great numbers' (W Berry, unpublished notes). Grierson (1962), however, records 1200 pairs of Common Terns nesting at Scotscraig in 1920 and almost double that number in 1921. This species tends to nest on inland moors, so although they are less threatened by high tides and sand drift than the next species, they are more vulnerable to afforestation. Subsequent to the planting of trees, they therefore moved to Earlshall where 1000 pairs nested in 1930, rising to 2000 pairs in 1936 'and still increasing'. Many terns had just started to nest in 1942, when practice-shooting over their nest sites caused the whole colony to desert and breeding practically ceased until 1950 (Grierson 1962). Numbers fluctuated greatly during the 1950s and 1960s, reaching a maximum of 200 pairs in 1953, and 300 pairs were recorded in 1973 (*Scottish Bird Report*). Since the 1980s, however, only 2–3 pairs have nested, all without success (*Fife Bird Reports*).

Arctic Terns were considered to have colonised the area more recently than the previous species, though Boase (1964) states that they were first recorded in 1885, and W Berry took a party to see them in 1905 when a few were shot for identification purposes (W Berry, unpublished notes). No early figures for nesting pairs exist, but, from 1914, a few nests were found annually, rising to 30 pairs in 1919 (Boase 1964). Breeding on or very close to the beach, this species suffered particularly heavily at the hands of the egg collectors and also from sand drift and flooding. In 1924, the total number of nesting pairs at Scotscraig was thought to be 50, while after the move to Earlshall about 30 pairs nested in 1936 with possibly other pairs elsewhere. From 1949, numbers increased markedly and the Arctic Tern became the most common nesting tern on Tentsmuir in the 1950s, peaking with 500 pairs in 1953 (Grierson 1962). In 1973, 175 attempted to breed, but not a single chick was fledged due to disturbance and flooding, and since the 1980s only 2–3 pairs have attempted to nest, without success (*Scottish Bird Reports*; *Fife Bird Reports*).

Although Sandwich Terns were reported as regular summer visitors, and breeding had been suspected for some years, the first confirmed breeding record was in 1906 when 130 pairs were found nesting on Tentsmuir. From then on they bred almost annually, with numbers rising to 350 pairs in 1916 and 500 in 1927 (Sandeman 1963). Although numbers varied year by year, as with all other terns, 1000 pairs are thought to have bred at Shelly Point to the south in 1933, dropping drastically to a few pairs during the war and rising to 48 pairs in 1956 (Boase 1964). Five hundred pairs attempted breeding in 1968 and 120 pairs in 1974, but in spite of voluntary wardening not a single chick was reared in either year (*Scottish Bird Reports*). It is probable that no Sandwich Terns nested between 1980 and 1993 (*Fife Bird Reports*).

Little Terns, as noted earlier, bred regularly with between 15 and 20 nesting pairs until 1900, rising to 30 in 1906 (Grierson 1962; Boase 1964). This was at the 'arena' – the exit of a draining ditch at Tentsmuir Point. Breeding here stopped after 1924 but a small colony developed in some sand dunes along the east shore with a few clutches observed in the 1950s. In 1948 a few nested at Shelly Point increasing to about 70 pairs in 1953, and some may also have nested at Tentsmuir Point. Numbers declined through the 1970s and only 1–2 pairs attempted breeding in the 1980s (*Scottish Bird Reports*). However, in 1992 three pairs nested at Tentsmuir Point, while in 1993 as many as 23 pairs attempted breeding by Shelly Spit. This good news was received after this chapter was written, and it is hoped that this situation will continue.

Though Millais was unable to find any nests of Roseate Terns, this rare species did breed at Tentsmuir in 1927 with two nests among the Sandwich Terns, and again in 1936 with one clutch (Boase 1964), while an amazing 18–20 pairs nested in 1956 (Mylne 1962). One pair attempted breeding again at Tentsmuir in 1972 (*Scottish Bird Report)* but none has nested here since.

Many species of duck have nested on Tentsmuir, but the Eiders probably suffered more from afforestation than any other species. Eiders had been breeding on Tentsmuir since at least 1850, though ruthless persecution by egg collectors prevented more than the odd duckling from being hatched (J Berry 1939). Unfortunately we do not have early counts of nests but Millais (1913) found 10–20 broods successfully reared, following W Berry's protection, and in 1920 nests numbered over 100. John Berry considered that the 1000 male Eider Ducks he counted off St Andrews in May 1923 were probably all 'home bred' (J Berry 1939). By the mid-1930s the ducks had moved to Earlshall and numbers were reckoned to be comparable to those found earlier on the Scotscraig division. After the war, when some keepering was reinstated at Earlshall, at least 50 birds were 'sitting' on the moor, with others at Shelly Point and Tentsmuir Point. Many verbal accounts from people who visited the area in the 1950s and 1960s tell of the large numbers of Eiders on Earlshall, with nests everywhere, and in 1971–72 a detailed survey was conducted, when it was estimated that 1500–1800 pairs bred in the Tentsmuir-St Andrews area (Pounder 1974). The forthcoming *Fife Breeding Bird Atlas,* a survey for which was carried out from 1991 to 1995, found about 20 nests in all in the Tentsmuir area from 1991 to 1993.

Shelduck also suffered severely from the afforestation. They were recorded as being very numerous on Scotscraig, with others nesting at Kinshaldy and Earlshall prior to World War One, but there are no counts. Grierson states that these birds were slower to make the move to Earlshall than the previous species. However, a census in 1954 showed that between 150 and 200 pairs nested on Earlshall with other pairs at Tentsmuir and Shelly Point (Grierson 1962). In 1974 there were still an estimated 130 pairs breeding here (*Scottish Bird Reports*), while the survey for the forthcoming *Fife Breeding Bird Atlas* found a maximum of 20 pairs from 1991 to 1993.

Of the wading birds, W Berry regarded Redshank to be very common and breeding in any suitable marshy ground. In the 1950s, Grierson found not less than twelve pairs on Earlshall and the coastal strips and up to ten pairs at Morton Lochs, making at least 20 pairs. None now nests.

Snipe were also regarded a common breeder, and according to W Berry used to breed all over Tentsmuir before afforestation (W Berry, unpublished notes). Since then they were known to breed freely around Morton Lochs and also on Earlshall with about 15 pairs, probably giving a total of 30 or so pairs in the 1950s (Grierson 1962). In 1994, North East Fife Ranger Service found a total of three, possibly four pairs, all on Earlshall (L Hatton, *pers. comm.*).

Ringed Plover were never regarded as an abundant breeder here, but a total of 50 pairs was recorded by Grierson in 1953. Since the 1960s, however, disturbance by people, dogs and bikes has reduced breeding success, with few young being reared, though seven pairs reared 18 young at the Goosepools in 1992 (*Fife Bird Report*).

After this sad catalogue of decline, it must be said that afforestation has also brought about some gains. In the last 40 years there has been an increase in Woodcock, Willow Warbler and Goldfinch; Siskin and Green Woodpecker now breed regularly; Crossbills breed occasionally and two new species have bred, Golden Oriole (twice), and Spotted Crake (once).

The following tables (4.1, 4.2, 4.3) are intended to demonstrate the changes in the bird population more clearly. Due to the difficulty of ensuring that like is compared with like, a simple method of presenting maximum figures within a suitable period has been adopted.

Table 4.1

a) Breeding Ducks

	1880–1919	1920–49	1950–79	1980–93
Regular Breeders				
Eider	50+ prs	250 prs	1500–1800 prs	20 prs
Shelduck	'very numerous'	'large numbers'	150–200 prs	20 prs (holding territories)
Mallard	regular	*c.* 40 prs	*c.* 40 prs	20 prs?
Tufted Duck	3–4 prs	3–4 prs	12 prs	2–3 prs?
Teal	10 prs	bred	18 prs	0?
Shovleer	1–2 prs	2–3 prs	2–3 prs	0
Occasional Breeders				
Gadwall	bred (1918)	?	bred? (1960)	?
Wigeon	bred? (1911)	bred? (1922)	bred (1953)	0
Pintail	?	?	bred? (1953)	0
Common Scoter		bred at least once (1947)		0
Scaup	bred? (1880)			

b) Breeding Waders

	1880–1919	1920–49	1950–79	1980–93
Dunlin	26 prs	10 prs (last 1937)	0	0
Golden Plover	3–4 prs	last 1938	0	0
Redshank	'fair density'	12 prs	18–20 prs	0
Snipe	'bred freely'	30 prs	20+ prs	3–4 prs
Ringed Plover	'very numerous'		50 prs	4–5 prs?
Lapwing	'common'	25 prs	25 prs	5–6 prs?
Curlew	'common'	4 prs	17 prs	3–4 prs?
Woodcock	?	1–2 prs	3-4 prs	increasing 20+ prs?

c) Breeding Terns

	1880–1919	1920–49	1950–79	1980–93
Sandwich Tern	*c.* 300 prs	*c.* 1000 prs	500 prs	2 prs?
Commom Tern	'considerable numbers'	2000+ prs	*c.* 300 prs	2 prs 1992 in 'NE Fife' all failed
Arctic Tern	a few prs	*c.* 50 prs	*c.* 500 prs	3 prs 1992 in 'NE Fife' all failed
Little Tern	30 prs	16+ prs	70+ prs	23 prs 1993*
Roseate Tern	1–3 prs	2–3 prs	18–20 prs	0
Black-Headed Gull	50 prs	*c.* 1000 prs	*c.* 8000 prs	0–1

* data received after the chapter was written.

Table 4.2: Tentsmuir – Lost Breeding Species

Lost by 1960:
Red Grouse
Black Grouse
Corncrake
Golden Plover
Dunlin
Magpie
Whinchat
Tree Sparrow?
Hooded Crow

Lost by 1993:
Teal
Shoveler
Redshank
Sandwich Tern
Roseate Tern
Wheatear
Stonechat
Corn Bunting

Probably lost by 1993:
Capercaillie (1 bird seen 1993)
Black-headed Gull (1 pr may have bred 1992)

Other Breeding Species which have declined in numbers:
Moorhen
Cuckoo
Redpoll

Table 4.3: Tentsmuir – Gains in the last 30 years

New species which breed regularly:
Siskin
Green Woodpecker

New species which breed occasionally:
Crossbill
Golden Oriole (twice)
Spotted Crake (once)

Species with increased population:
Woodcock
Willow Warbler
Carrion Crow
Goldfinch

Comparison of developments in the bird population of Tentsmuir with those at a very similar locality is of interest. There are not many such sites on the east coast of Scotland, but the Sands of Forvie–Ythan estuary complex north of Aberdeen, bears similarities with the old Tentsmuir in a number of ways: both border the North Sea and both consist largely of sand dunes and heather moor. Unlike Tentsmuir these habitats have been retained at the Ythan and, importantly, it has also escaped forestry plantations on a large scale. Public access to the area where the terns breed is restricted during the breeding season. This is enforced by temporary fencing which, however, cannot keep out foxes. Both the Ythan and the Sands of Forvie have also been important as roosts for wintering geese, especially Pink-footed Geese.

So what is the case now? (Tables 4.4, 4.5.) Eiders breed in numbers on the Ythan and Sands of Forvie (about 800 pairs), though with declining success recently, while the Shelduck population is stable with over 80 breeding pairs. Four species of terns still breed, the Sandwich Tern in very substantial numbers (1500 pairs), while with 50 pairs of Little Terns it is a nationally important breeding place for this species. Geese still roost on the Ythan and the hinterland during the winter in their thousands, whereas they have deserted Tentsmuir Point since the 1960s, probably due to nearby flying activities from RAF Leuchars. Although numbers are not available for breeding Redshank, Snipe and Ringed Plover, the present warden says that the population of each of these is stable and healthy (B Davis, *pers. comm.*).

Table 4.4: The Ythan Estuary and Sands of Forvie

Some Breeding Species

	1880–1919	1920–1949	1950–1979	1980–1993
Eider	first 1885 'abundant'	*c.* 800 prs	2015 prs	*c.* 1500 prs
Shelduck	'increasing'	*c.* 40 prs	80 prs	70 prs
Teal	bred	bred	stable	stable? 10 prs
Sandwich Tern			1500 prs	1500 prs
Common Tern		1000+ prs	150 prs	150 prs
Arctic Tern			160 prs	150 prs
Little Tern			50 prs	50 prs
Roseate Tern			1–2 prs	
Black-Headed Gull			570 prs	500+ prs

Table 4.5 (from Thom 1986)

	1969–70	1970–74	1974–79	1980–8
SANDWICH TERN:				
Sands of Forvie	740 prs	1056 prs	1194 prs	1671 prs
Tentsmuir	-	-	-	-
COMMON TERN:				
Sands of Forvie	475 prs	351 prs	320 prs	465 prs
Tentsmuir	-	-	-	-
ARCTIC TERN:				
Sands of Forvie	172 prs*	202 prs*		
Tentsmuir	A great colony of 500 prs in 1953 – few breed now			

LITTLE TERN:	1971	'72	'73	'74	'75	'76	'77	'78	'79	'80	'81	'82	'83	'84
Sands of Forvie	11	4	4	8	17	80	69	51	60	50	46	54	32	4
Tentsmuir	10	?	24	16	?	18	10	—	—	0–5 prs	—	—	—	—

* from Buckland *et al.* (1990)

The University of Aberdeen has a field station at Culterty next to the Ythan, from which extensive research programmes are carried out, and a warden is employed by SNH to look after this important wildlife area. A detailed account of the ornithological interest of the Sands of Forvie and the Ythan complex was published in *Scottish Birds* (1965, 5, pp. 219–35), and another in *Scottish Bird News* 1991.

Today, thousands of people visit both the Aberdeenshire and Fife areas for the enjoyment of sea and scenery, to watch the wildlife and to pursue recreational purposes. Few of the people who visit Tentsmuir and enjoy the forest walks will know of the enormous changes which have taken place so recently; only the sandhills and heather among the pine trees act as reminders of a past landscape. So the answer to the question posed in the title to this chapter has sadly proved to be in the affirmative: there has been an ecological catastrophe, at least as far as the birds are concerned. Nevertheless, a positive note should be struck. Although so little now remains of the once extensive Tentsmuir, it is encouraging to note that in spring 1994, which was very wet, a flush appeared on Earlshall which remained for several months and immediately attracted a number of interesting species, such as a pair of Garganey, up to 26 Little Gulls, and a Wood Sandpiper, while several Lapwing and Common Snipe were displaying. More than 20 male Eider were seen on the flush and six pairs of Shelduck. This demonstrates what could be the case if water could be retained on a more permanent basis.

Bibliography

Anderson, A, 'Birdwatching around the Ythan estuary, Newburgh, Aberdeenshire', *Scottish Bird News*, 24 (1991)

Baxter, E V and Rintoul, E L, *The Birds of Scotland* (Oliver and Boyd, 1953)

Berry, J, *The Status and Distribution of Wild Geese and Wild Duck in Scotland* (CUP, 1939)

Berry, W, 'On the introduction of Grouse to the Tentsmuir in Fife', *Annals of Scottish Natural History,* 12 (1894), pp. 197–203

Boase, Henry, 'The Birds of North Fife' (unpublished manuscript in the Waterston Library, SOC, 21 Regent Terrace, Edinburgh, EG7 5BT; 1994)

Buckland, S T, Bell, M V and Picozzi, N, *The Birds of North-East Scotland* (The North-East Scotland Bird Club, Aberdeen, 1990)

Dalgleish, R, 'Parish of Ferry-Port-on-Craig', *The Statistical Account of Scotland,* X, ed. Sinclair, Sir J (1796). Edition of 1978 by Cant, R G

Dunnet, G M, Milne, H, Young, C M, Goss-Custard, J D, Patterson, J J and Anderson, A, 'Research at Culterty Field Station', *Scottish Birds*, 3 (1965), pp. 219–23

Fife Bird Reports 1980–1993

Grierson, J, 'A Check-list of the Birds of Tentsmuir', *Scottish Birds,* 2 (special supplement, 1962), pp. 113–64

Harvie-Brown, J A, *A Fauna of the Tay Basin and Strathmore* (Oliver & Boyd, 1906)

Kettle, M, 'Parish of Leuchars', *The Statistical Account of Scotland, X,* ed. Sinclair, Sir J (1796). Edition of 1978 by Cant, R G

Leslie Smith, T, 'Growth and Decline of an artificial Grouse Moor', *Scottish Naturalist*, 60 (1948), pp. 99–106

Mylne, C K, 'Roseate Terns Breeding on the Mainland of Fife in 1956', *Scottish Birds*, 2 (1962), pp. 286–93

Pounder, H, 'Breeding and Moulting Eider in the Tay Region', *Scottish Birds*, 8 (1974), pp. 159–76

Sandeman, G L, 'Roseate and Sandwich Tern Colonies in the Forth and Neighbouring Areas',

Scottish Birds, 2 (1963), pp. 286–93
Scottish Bird Reports, 1968–1980
Thom, V, *The Birds in Scotland* (Poyser, 1986)
Wilson, J H, *Rambles round St Andrews* (Henderson & Son, University Press, St Andrews, 1910)

Acknowledgements

Dr John Berry kindly let me have a copy of his father, William Berry's, unpublished List of the Birds observed at Tayfield and adjacent farms' (including Tentsmuir) 1872–1947, as well as a note from J F P Keddie on 'Tentsmuir and the changes that have affected nesting Terns' dated 1973, but best of all are the first-hand information and fascinating details he has passed on to me in conversation about Tentsmuir. I also gratefully acknowledge information and data from staff at SNH, North East Fife Ranger Service and Culterty Field Station.

5

The Management Plans of Tentsmuir Point National Nature Reserve

Thomas Huxley

Introduction: The Historical Background

The Nature Conservancy came into being by Royal Charter in 1949, and its small scientific staff in Scotland, under the Director (Scotland) John Berry, was joined by the late Dr J W Eggeling who held the post of Conservation Officer (Scotland). In October of the following year, the writer was recruited as Eggeling's assistant. Some months thereafter, with Dr J M Boyd and N J Gordon having arrived at Hope Terrace, Eggeling organised his conservation team into four regions: Boyd, responsible for the Western Highlands and Islands; Grant Roger (one of the earlier recruited team of scientists), the Eastern Highlands; Nancy Gordon, the remaining eastern counties north of the Forth, along with Caithness, Sutherland, Shetland and Orkney; and Thomas Huxley, Southern Scotland. The four held the post of Regional Officer, a title that had been created in England several years earlier. Each was responsible for National Nature Reserves (NNRs) that had by that time been created. Eggeling, however, chose for the time being to retain direct responsibility for the Fife reserves at Tentsmuir Point and the nearby Morton Lochs, although they were nominally in Nancy Gordon's area, because, as he put it, he 'wanted to keep his hand in' on some aspect of direct management. Another key person involved in reserve acquisition and management was the Land Agent for Scotland, The Hon. J C Arbuthnott, later to become Viscount Arbuthnott and Chairman of the Scottish Committee of the Nature Conservancy Council.

Today, following the merger in 1992 of the Nature Conservancy Council and the Countryside Commission for Scotland into Scottish Natural Heritage with its staff of about 600, some effort is required to recall the small size of the Nature Conservancy in its early years. Many procedures now taken for granted had to be initiated as novel, management plans for National Natural Reserves being a case in point. Before returning to Scotland, Dr Eggeling had served in the Colonial Forest Service in Uganda and Tanganyika and in that profession it was standard practice to have forest management plans prepared for each forest, not only so as to ensure that everyone involved in managing a forest worked to a commonly agreed plan, but also to secure continuity of policies and budgets in the event of changes in personnel. The same procedure, he proposed, was required for NNRs.

Accordingly, at about the time the four regional Officers were settling into their new duties, Dr Eggeling set out a one-page Proforma for NNR management plans. The plan could be considered as falling into three sections: Chapters I to IV being descriptive, Chapter V the objects of management, and the remaining chapters prescriptive, i.e. setting out what had to be done to satisfy the objects of management. There was also a bibliography and one or more appendices for including copies or summaries of the legal conditions under which the area had been 'declared' as a NNR, either by purchase, lease or agreement with the owner; byelaws where they existed; annual expenditure; and, notionally very important but later too often overlooked, 'Conclusions drawn from work done'. The plan period was five years; from the outset it was recognised that circumstances at reserves could change and that management plans would need to be revised at regular intervals.

Recently, Marren (1994) has described the common pattern of NNR management plans dating from 1983, prepared under the guidance of a detailed handbook, the pivotal central section being much more detailed than in Eggeling's 1956 proforma. At that time, objects of management were seen as having a close relationship to the reasons for acquisition. By 1983, however, the central section of the plan had become a crucial chapter for debate of pros and cons:

> The second section attempts to evaluate the relative importance of the Reserve, both in general terms and in the more detailed aspects of its flora, fauna and physiology. It also specifies what would be desirable in a more ideal world, and then goes on to list the obligations and constraints that limit what can be done in practice. This section forms the intellectual and scientific justification for what happens on the reserve. It includes a reasoned review of the options: does the habitat need management? If so, should the latter be limited in extent or thorough-going? Are there special species that need individual attention? And how does one cater for a range of habitats, all of them in the process of perpetual change? (Marren 1994)

As Marren comments, this crucial part of the new type management plan, even if it achieved nothing else, did at least force managers to think carefully about their aims. In retrospect, it is interesting that the Conservancy's early plans generally did not, in the actual written plans themselves, enter into much discussion about objects of management, albeit there was often considerable debate amongst staff. A possible explanation may have been a reluctance to present our masters with an array of propositions debating whether the simplistic reasons for reserve acquisition and management were both realisable and not unacceptably costly. To have done so could, perhaps, have suggested some doubts as to whether we really understood what we were proposing to do and, in the early days, being uncertain was not politically constructive. The precautionary principle had yet to be promoted! Another less controversial explanation is that it is not possible to understand a reserve fully other than by knowing it over a period of time, however good the initial survey of the flora and fauna. The fact that such basic survey was poor – other than for birds and sometimes flowering plants and generally a blank page for invertebrates – was also a serious drawback. Much more importantly, our understanding of ecological processes on reserves for the long-term securing of their conservation interest was in its infancy because this requires research over time and, for the early management plans, that commodity was inevitably lacking.

For an NNR management plan to be approved and thereby assign to its prescription some degree of forward financial commitment, it had to be agreed by the Scottish Advisory Committee. In practice, of course, this commitment was both notionally binding and fictional because actual expenditure on a reserve, within the period of a plan, frequently depended on the Conservancy's overall annual allocation and on competing priorities. However, before plans were presented to the Scottish Committee, they were considered by a type of peer group review, called the Conservation Group, which met in London under the Chairmanship of Dr Barton Worthington, whose skilful and kindly guidance of the debates has received, in this writer's view, inadequate recognition in accounts of the Conservancy's early history. The Group comprised all the Regional Officers and Land Agents throughout Britain and, depending on the reserve management plan being considered, several representatives of scientific teams, and it provided an important opportunity for shared consideration of reserve management objectives. To the extent that any group of scientists and land managers in Britain at that time understood the long-term ecological implications of what was being done on reserves, it is probably fair to observe that there was no other group with more experience, albeit there were surely other ecologists with different opinions.

In its debates, the Conservation Group also provided, at that time, a uniquely invaluable opportunity for mutual education. For example, the writer has never forgotten the impact of a contribution from James Hemsley, then the Regional Officer for South Central England, in presenting his Management Plan for Kingley Vale in West Sussex. The thrust of Hemsley's case related to the importance of knowing about land use history; that unless one had thoroughly researched past influences and conditions at a reserve, one could become badly unstuck in deciding how to plan for its future conservation.

The first use of Eggeling's proforma for NNR management was at Morton Lochs, prepared jointly with Arbuthnott in December 1956 and approved by the Scottish Committee in April of the following year. A management plan had been drafted for Yarner Wood in Devon two years earlier, so possibly the only priority claim for the Morton Lochs plan was in regard to it having provided a practical model, in terms of overall layout, followed by all GB NNR plans until the 1980s. The Eggeling-Arbuthnott plan for Tentsmuir Point NNR followed soon after, its preparation being completed in January 1957 and its approval by the Scottish Committee at the same meeting as for Morton Lochs, in April of that year.

In summarising the first and subsequent plans for Tentsmuir, there are many extracts taken from the text, generally without punctuated attribution, for ease of reading. Much, of course, has been omitted, especially where sections, in the writer's opinion, are not of special relevance to the issues raised at the Battleby conference. The writer has not delved into the files and other reports contemporary with the date of the plans described. They would have contained some interesting insights not deducible from the management plans themselves. For example, in 1978, or thereabouts, Dr R D Fairley wrote a critique of Tentsmuir management at the conclusion of his period as summer warden that the writer has read but not made use of and Nancy Gordon has told me that at a meeting of the British Association at Dundee in 1968 there was a session devoted to Tentsmuir. It is stressed, therefore, that all that follows has been extracted solely from the Tentsmuir Point management plan file.

The First Management Plan for Tentsmuir Point NNR

The reserve was acquired by purchase from the Forestry Commission (92 acres for

£120 in 1954), in fulfilment of an undertaking by the Commission to the Dundee Naturalists' Society that if the latter relinquished all rights to an 80-acre area at Tentsmuir, previously set aside as a bird sanctuary, Tentsmuir Point would be made available as a nature reserve. It was declared a NNR in March 1954.

The primary interest of the reserve was stated as physiographical, because more land was here being won from the sea by natural means, perhaps more rapidly than in any other part of Britain. (This was the view at the time; in later years the rate of accretion slowed significantly. cf. Chapter 1.) Associated with this accretion, there was a considerable ecological and botanical interest. The rapid enlargement of the ground afforded abundant opportunity for observing and studying the processes of colonisation and succession – in which strand and dune plants tolerant of saline conditions, plants of brackish water and plants of light soils were all involved. In Eggeling's own hand, he added that 'colonisation by invertebrates offers an equally important subject for study'.

Additional interests were zoological: sea duck frequenting the foreshore waters and the Abertay sands being a roost for migratory geese in appropriate seasons. At low tide, the Sands were also well known as a resting place for large numbers of common seals.

In retrospect, it is curious that the plan does not state that 'part of Tentsmuir, including Morton Lochs' was recommended as a nature reserve by the Scottish Wild Life Conservation Committee (Cmd 7814). This was the committee, under the Chairmanship of Professor James Ritchie, that had been set up in 1946 by the Scottish National Parks Committee under J D Ramsay. The report listing nature reserves, published in 1949, was the final report of the two committees. Dr J Berry and F F Darling were also members of the Wild Life and Conservation Committee.

Regarding Tentsmuir, the report states:

> The land lying on the seaward side of the present limit of planting by the Forestry Commission consists mainly of sand dunes and flats, and provides examples of the various stages in dune formation and their colonisation by plants. Incursions by high tides result in the formation of salt pans. The local development of willow scrub is the habitat of a distinctive insect life.

Also, in retrospect, the non-technical language of both descriptions is interesting, albeit one can only speculate whether this reflected the authors' states of knowledge or a policy to keep things simple. For example, although jumping well ahead in time, the Nature Conservation Review (Ratcliffe 1977) describes Tentsmuir Dunes as having 'an actively aggrading lime-poor dune system with full seral succession from embryo slacks and dunes to alder, birch and willow scrub. The site has the best population of *Elymus arenarius* in Britain and notable abundance of *Astragalus danicus*, *Corallorhiza trifida*, *Empetrum nigrum* and *Juncus balticus*. Lichen-rich dwarf scrub heaths are well represented on the stable dunes'. Incidentally, although the NCR review states that over 400 species of flowering plants have been recorded, this figure relates to the whole Tentsmuir area; for the reserve itself the number is nearer 320 (Kinnear *pers. comm.*).

In Chapter III, Eggeling's description of the shoreline changes is of particular interest. Throughout the past hundred years, land had continued to extend eastwards along the whole of the east-facing shore of the northern portion of Tentsmuir. During this time, the zone of maximum accretion had steadily shifted towards Tentsmuir

Point, such that the shoreline had swung to face a little more south of east than formerly. Some time between 1905 and 1915, a sand dune began to develop on the foreshore east of the then high water mark. New dunes accumulated on its northern side and a foredune grew northwards parallel to the old shoreline. In 1956 the process was still continuing. The long ridges running parallel with the shore within the forestry plantations may have originated in a similar way to the aforementioned foredune. Eggeling's description includes a variety of evidence as to the causes of this accretion, his sources including Admiralty charts dating from 1833 and changes in ship movements entering the Tay, the possible effects of wartime defence works and studies carried out by A T Grove in the 1950s. Regarding the important effects of the Forestry Commission plantations dating from 1920, Eggeling wrote that they 'may have reduced the strength of off-shore winds, thereby hastening the accumulation of sand blowing from the drying inter-tidal sands'.

The crucial Chapter V dealt with Objects of Management and these were stated as follows:

1. to retain the area in such a state that changes of coastline, formation of new dunes and slacks and their colonisation by vegetation may be studied;
2. measure coastal accretion and, as opportunity permits, investigate the processes which cause it; and
3. encourage ecological and geomorphological studies within the reserve.

Ancillary objects were to include biological survey, with periodic assessments, and the maintenance of adequate records.

The policies to be adopted in satisfaction of these objectives were fairly simple. Regarding the first aim, a warden was required to maintain the area in an unspoilt condition 'to see that no threats to the area develop'. Objective 2 was limited to the erection of two lines of posts at right angles to the coast, their position to be carefully surveyed and the height of their exposed portions to be measured at regular intervals. This prescription was on the recommendation of the Conservancy's physiographer because it should provide some basic information on which a fuller study could be based. A detailed physiographical study of Tentsmuir was not envisaged within the period of the plan, 'desirable though such an investigation is... because of a full programme (of the physiographical section) elsewhere', Objective 3 would happen when suitable persons 'turn up' who would be encouraged to do research in the reserve.

These policies were fairly typical of the Conservancy's early management plans. Outstanding areas were acquired as NNRs and an array of interesting research subjects identified but thereafter little actually done because of lack of resources and/or competing priorities.

On one matter, however, the first management plan for Tentsmuir NNR was determined and specific. The western portion of the reserve was considered extremely liable to colonisation by conifers from seed from the adjoining plantations. The planted species were chiefly exotic. Scots pine was also involved and, although almost certainly native to the area, Eggeling did not judge this species to be a normal component of the early stages of colonisation of newly formed dunes. Therefore it was to be part of the reserve policy that:

a. all exotic trees will continue to be weeded out of the reserve; and
b. all Scots pine seedlings and saplings will be weeded out also, except in a

control area (specified in the plan) extending to one fifth of the reserve.

Weeding parties were sometimes organised at weekends with the Eggeling family and dogs. The writer recalls taking part in one of these when he was given a vivid explanation of the series of war-time beach defences. In one of the plan's appendices, Eggeling recorded that total conifer seedlings uprooted by the end of 1958 were 5453 and 4355 in 1959/60, by which time a thick pine cover was already spreading over parts of the control area. By 1961 studies of the reserve had been initiated by the Botany Department of St Andrews University (under Professor Burnett) and a start made on a detailed levelling survey of the reserve by the Geography Department (under J H Paterson).

The Second Management Plan for Tentsmuir Point NNR

In accordance with the plan period of five years, a first revision (called here the Second Plan) was due in 1961. As so frequently happened, and perhaps still does, pressure of other work delayed matters and the second plan did not go before the Scottish Committee until June 1963. By that time several things had happened. First, as well as the original 92 acres bought from the Forestry Commission, two small additional areas had been purchased, also from the Commission, and in the same year (1962), by agreement with the Crown Estate Commissioners, the reserve was extended to include the foreshore and Abertay Sands. Also in 1962, the reserve became the subject of byelaws, mainly to control shooting and collecting but also to control landing on the seaward part of the reserve. Another change was that before the end of the first plan period, Eggeling had become so involved in the Conservancy's increasing work throughout Scotland, that he had relinquished his self-elected responsibilities for the Fife reserves to the Regional Officer and thus preparation of the second plan fell to Nancy Gordon.

As befitting her training as a geographer, the second plan was prefaced by a substantial general introduction to dunes of conservation importance in Scotland. The twelve areas selected to illustrate different types of dune systems ranged from Dunnet Bay in Caithness to Torrs Warren in Wigtonshire and from Eoligarry on Barra to St Cyrus and Tentsmuir on the east coast. This masterly summary was written fourteen years before Mather and Ritchie (1977) at Aberdeen had published their review of the beaches of the Highlands and Islands of Scotland, and it concluded:

> Ranwell (1955) has described Tentsmuir Point in relation to Newborough Warren
> and seven other dune systems in England and Wales. It is hoped that this general
> introduction will be expanded to cover dune reserves in the whole of Britain.

The NCR described 137 coastal sites, including a substantial number of dune systems. Gordon's hope was therefore bound to take many years to be fulfilled and the good news, so the writer is informed (Fairley *pers. comm.*) is that it soon will be in Scotland through contracts commissioned by Scottish Natural Heritage, due to be published in 1996.

In the second plan, the primary interests were categorised as both physiographical and botanical, deriving from the 'exceptionally rapid sand accretion and growth of the coastline'. Reference is made to its earlier listing in Cmd 7814 and regarding additional interests, the importance of the Abertay Sands, which by 1963 had been ranked as a National Wildfowl Refuge. The descriptive chapter now runs to four times the length of the first plan and there are many references to research done in the reserve, for example on soil chemistry. In a section on factors that have guided the process of colonisation and the types of dune and slack vegetation, as well as climate and soil, afforestation is listed: the plantations having 'provided an increasing amount of shelter to the Reserve and probably lowered the water table'.

In the section on fauna, the plan states that 'there are no longer rabbits on the reserve'. Numbers were kept down after the reduction by myxomatosis in 1955 and they were finally eliminated in 1960, since when the brown hare had greatly increased. Regarding birds, although over 100 species had been recorded as seen within the reserve, within the area of Tentsmuir generally 'afforestation had brought many changes in the bird population' (see Chapter 4).

In the section on land use history, there is rather more detail than in the first plan about the use of the area during the Second World War and it includes the enigmatic statement that the 'Air Ministry intend to relinquish their use of the land within the reserve in the near future'.

Essentially, the objects of management in the second plan were unchanged. They were:

1. to retain the area in an undisturbed state in order that coastline changes and natural colonisation processes can be studied;
2. to measure coastal accretion or erosion and investigate the reason for it;
3. to encourage ecological studies; and
4. to ensure minimal disturbance of the foreshore and Abertay Sands so that wildfowl will continue to visit them and to protect the nest-sites of sea-birds.

In fulfilment of these objectives, part-time wardening was reinforced in the winter months by the full-time presence of Malcolm Smith, a skilled amateur entomologist, one of several part-time and honorary wardens who contributed valuable information about the reserve. The Conservancy's cash flow still did not permit the appointment of a full-time warden, despite the importance of ensuring that the newly enacted byelaws were observed. The extensive colonisation by conifers continued to be considered a major problem and the policy of weeding out the exotics throughout the reserve and Scots pine from all but the control area was restated. All the rest of the plan's prescriptions deal with research and are essentially a list of work at the time being done in the reserve by students from several universities. There is rather more in the second plan about public access, at which time there were no rights of way through the Forestry Commission's plantations.

The Third Management Plan for Tentsmuir Point NNR

Ten years elapsed before a third plan was drafted in 1973 by one of the Region's assistant regional officers, Dr Rosalind A H Smith. Much shorter than the second plan, it was produced to form a basis for the urgent decisions and management activities that had to be undertaken during the next five years. Although the reasons for the establishment were unchanged and the reader reminded of the objects of management as stated in the 1963 plan, Smith observed that these objects effectively precluded taking action to limit the spread of invasive species, such as Scots pine and sea-buck-thorn (*Hippophaë rhamnoides*) and thus, if adhered to strictly, they would hazard the conservation interests of important components of the reserve. It was proposed, therefore, that the objects be re-phrased to take into account the conservation interests of the reserve as they were perceived at that time. The re-phrased objects of management were:

1. to conserve the variety of habitats and species characteristic of the reserve and relating to its position in the national series of sand dune reserves, insofar as this can be achieved while allowing the physiographical development of the dune system and the parallel successional stages of colonisation by native species of plant and animal life to take place with minimum interference.
2. to carry out and encourage research into the physiography and ecology of the dune system; and
3. to conserve the wildlife interest of Abertay Sands by the prevention of disturbance.

The first set of management prescriptions thus dealt with the invasive species in terms much more draconian than those in preceding plans. The 'control' area had, by 1973, become woodland and natural regeneration was so advanced over another compartment, that removal of the young trees was considered unacceptable 'without damage to the habitat'. Colonisation by sea-buckthorn, 'introduced into Tentsmuir by the Forestry Commission', formed dense thickets in the southern part of the reserve. The upshot of these changes was to recommend more elimination of seedlings over certain areas and the elimination of sea-buckthorn in others, while allowing this colonisation to take its course elsewhere.

Rabbits had also returned to become a major problem since 1960 when they had 'been finally eliminated'. The effects of their considerable increase had been the virtual elimination of scrub vegetation in the slacks, of lichen heath and several rare species and the dominance over much of the drier mature dune area of rose-bay willow-herb (*Chamaenerion angustifolium*). The erection of rabbit-proof fences and elimination of rabbits within the areas thus enclosed, in combination with regulation of numbers elsewhere, were the management action proposed in accordance with a recommended policy of maintaining a variety of habitats within the reserve, from ungrazed to lightly and heavily grazed communities.

The second management plan's tentative reference to the drying out of some of the slacks was also identified as a subject for action in the third plan because 'a drainage channel cut by the Forestry Commission in 1957 has substantially increased the rapidity with which an important burn dried out'. Following discussions with the Forestry Commission, it was proposed therefore to install a sluice in the Forestry Commission's drain so as to redirect water back into the reserve 'while at the same time avoiding floodback into the Forestry Commission's land'. An increase in wardening resources was needed to cope with increased public use of the reserve. New reserve signs were also required but had to await revision of the map of the foreshore and sandbanks so as to enable revision of the byelaws.

Policies and Prescriptions, 1984–89

The management plan file contains a draft five-page list of policies and prescriptions for the period 1984 to 1989 prepared by another assistant regional officer S J Leach in association with the full-time warden P K Kinnear, who also had duties elsewhere. The draft on file is dated 3.4.85. This is a detailed setting out of management policies and work programmes, grouped under nine policy headings and, in total, over 80 specific tasks. The last policy (the authors were ever hopeful) was to provide adequate staff to carry out the first eight. The document conveyed a strong sense of urgency about maintaining the *status quo* over much of the landward part of the reserve and even manipulating succession where particular plant communities are at risk of being lost, especially nationally rare plant communities. Thus, in addition to continuing with the removal of conifers, sea-buckthorn and birch, willow (*Salix cinerea* and other large *Salix* spp) were to be removed from certain wet slacks. Pumps, as well as sluices, were to be used to enhance flooding. It is in this document that the writer has found the first reference to initiating the trial use of domestic stock to control scrub growth while, in regard to the more persistently invasive scrub species, both stump treatment and spraying re-growth with herbicides were prescribed. Most of the other tasks concerned much more rigorous monitoring and autoecological studies of plant and animal species of conservation importance, enough to keep several university departments occupied for decades.

The Fourth Management Plan for Tentsmuir Point NNR

In 1991 an ecological consultant, Alan Booth, drafted a fourth plan, notionally for the Tayport–Tentsmuir Site of Special Scientific Interest (SSSI), renotified in 1983 under the 1981 Wildlife and Countryside Act, but in practice a joint plan for the Morton Lochs and Tentsmuir Point NNRs. Booth carried out this work in consultation with local staff. The plan's layout followed the guidance notes described by Marren (1994) encouraging managers to think about aims. Homing in on the section headed 'Past Management for Nature Conservation', the author observed that, although the reserve was originally regarded as a high value site for research into the natural processes of accretion, erosion and succession, twenty years later scrub invasion had become such a strong threat to the diversity of plant communities that stronger measures had had to be prescribed in the third plan and the 1984 policy document. These, in Booth's opinion, seemed to have been at least partially successful, for example that since the mid-eighties much of the pine had been removed from the reserve, attempts to control the birch had been continued and the sea-buckthorn largely eradicated.

Because Booth's contract related to the SSSI, he quoted from the description of the site accompanying the formal notification papers: 'Tentsmuir is a key geomorphological site for the study of active beach and coastal processes [having] considerable potential for studies of the processes and development of coastal progradation and… interaction of vegetation. [The] extraordinary diversity of sand dune vegetation and the large number of vascular plant species includes many national or regional rarities'. In his evaluation of the site, he observed that the relatively small size of Tentsmuir results in it being particularly vulnerable to the effects of adjacent land management, such as drainage, aerial spraying and spread of tree seed. Under the heading of 'naturalness', similar comments were made in regard to the proximity of the commercial plantations, adding 'shading along the western edge of the reserve' as another effect. Interestingly, having regard to earlier observations about rabbit numbers [absent in 1963 and abundant in 1973], Booth noted the drop in grazing pressure from rabbits following myxomatosis in 1955 had led, as in many British dune systems, to rapid seral succession behind the yellow dunes to scrub vegetation.

Under a later 'fragility' sub-heading, there is an observation on the speedy succession of the plant communities of slacks, from salt marsh, through brackish, fen and mire communities, once isolated from tidal inundation and replacement of salt water by fresh. The author considered that the principal human impacts are through artificial drainage of adjacent forestry plantations and, for the same reason, the proximity of a large seed source. As to 'position in an ecological/geographic unit', he stated that the Tentsmuir reserve comprises only the seaward part of a once much larger system stretching inland and southwards to embrace what is now Earlshall Muir SSSI.

The management chapter lists 'ideal management objectives', much as stated in the 1973 plan and 1984 prescriptions. Under 'managerial constraints', the lack of a full-time warden dedicated solely to Tentsmuir was identified as making 'achievement of all of this site's potential difficult' and likewise the demise of the Manpower Services Community Programme on the ability to carry out estate work, such as scrub removal. In the section under the heading of 'operational objectives and management options: selection and ranking', Booth observed that ideal overall objectives had been compromised by the impacts listed earlier and that it was therefore essential to intervene in the natural processes in order to achieve these objectives. The rest of the plan considered a variety of intervention activities. For example, under 'winter flooding', Booth stated that although six previous winters had seen standing water on the reserve, the main long-term threat must be the lowering of the water table by agriculture and silviculture. He therefore suggested that negotiations should commence with the Forestry Commission to redirect overland flow through its drainage ditches or by extraction and pumping 'should the reserve be thought of sufficient value'. In a cautionary note, he added that nutrient content of the imported water could be too high and thus perhaps extraction by bore preferred. The plan debated the relative benefits and disadvantages of machine mowing rather than grazing to control scrub and that 'restoration of open dune by goat grazing seems to have been successful'. The plan also had much to say about recreational pressures and other conservation objectives, for example relating to birds and invertebrates.

Comments and Conclusions

In concluding this historical account of past management plans, it is important to recognise that history does not end with the fourth plan. Staff of the South East Region of Scottish Natural Heritage are currently engaged in preparing a fifth revision to the plan. Management is an ongoing operation and plans for Tentsmuir will continue to evolve in response to the Reserve's physiographical and ecological dynamics. Furthermore, although the writer has included names of authors of plans and a few other main players, readers should be aware that many other people in a variety of capacities as honorary wardens, have devoted much time to its care.

It is also helpful to recognise, as Booth observed at several points in his plan, that many of the management problems at Tentsmuir are not peculiar to it but have been experienced at many other British reserves, not all of which are coastal. For example, the ecological effects of the decline and rise in rabbit populations has been studied in many grassland reserves and there was at one time a special study group considering how to manage the rapid spread of sea-buckthorn (Ranwell 1972). Changes in water levels have also been a problem experienced on dozens of other reserves. Many examples of the actions taken to manipulate natural and man-made changes considered damaging to conservation interests are described in lively detail in Marren's book, nature reserve management having become 'one of the distinctive arts of the twentieth century... in which the maximum number of habitats are crammed within the confines of a small isolated reserve' (Marren 1994: 193). Sometimes there are no alternatives to what in another context would be described as gardening, with all that that implies for the horticultural management of soils, sward, water regime and labour and machinery costs.

There may be disagreement with some of the statements extracted from management plans about the cause of change. For example, at the Battleby conference, the writer recollects discussion about the effects of the Forestry Commission's plantations on the water regime of the reserve, in the course of which it was stated that under certain conditions salt water within the plantations could still be so high that drainage ditches ran full. The truth of that is not doubted, likewise that over a period of 40 years in the rapid growth of a coniferous forest, conduction of soil water from roots to needles and its evapotranspiration will have been immeasurably greater than had the lands remained unplanted, and that this will have had a significant effect on the adjoining land.

Some suggestions as to the management of land for conservation may be put forward:

1. Reserves acquired because they demonstrate ecological succession will probably eventually present an inherent dilemma for management because at a later stage people may want to retain the earlier mix of habitats and communities, and succession works against that aim.
2. A reserve selected as representing an array of habitats which formerly extended over a much larger area, part of which (especially when that part is adjacent to the reserve) has been much altered by human intervention, is highly likely to present formidable difficulties for the conservation of the original full range of habitats wholly within the reserved part.
3. At Tentsmuir, as at some other coastal reserves, there has been the fundamental limitation that the land acquired for reservation is a section (the seaward part) of what ideally would have been a succession of habitats stretching much further inland. Conservation management cannot therefore reach back inland.
4. Notwithstanding that specified courses of action command wide agreement, resources will often be insufficient to undertake the work adequately.
5. A tendency to delegate downwards responsibility for the drafting of management plans or even to put the work out to contract, while in no way reflecting on the plans themselves, may facilitate a distinct perspective amongst senior personnel which may blur whatever sense of urgency the plans were intended to convey.
6. Criticisms of past decisions, or inadequate resources to act on them, may overshadow considerable successes. Tentsmuir was made a reserve primarily because it 'afforded abundant opportunity for studying the processes of colonisation and

succession' and Booth listed over one hundred publications and research reports resulting from studies undertaken in the reserve.

7. For some readers, it may be thought that the writer has been carrying out vivisection without anaesthetic and they feel some discomfort. In truth, much invaluable experience has been gained from the management of the Tentsmuir Point NNR and this highly commendable fact should not be allowed to overshadow continuing debate about problems. Possibly, however, in any further stocktaking review of this experience, there could be benefit from learning more about how problems have been overcome at similar reserves elsewhere in Britain.

Bibliography

Cmd. 7814, *Final Report of the Scottish Wild Life Conservation Committee* (HMSO, 1949)

Marren, P, *England's National Nature Reserves* (English Nature; T & A D Poyser Natural History, 1994)

Mather, A S and Ritchie, W, *The Beaches of the Highlands and Islands of Scotland* (Countryside Commission for Scotland, 1977)

Ranwell, D S, 'Slack vegetation, dune system development and cyclical change at Newborough Warren, Anglesey' (Ph.D. thesis, University of London, 1955)

Ranwell, D S (ed.), *The management of Sea Buckthorn Hippophaë rhamnoides L. on selected sites in Great Britain* (report of the *Hippophaë* study group, Nature Conservancy, 1972)

Ratcliffe, D (ed.), *A Nature Conservation Review* (Cambridge University Press, 1977)

Acknowledgements

It is a pleasure to thank Professor T C Smout for the invitation to provide this contribution to this book. I am also indebted to the following for helpful comments and corrections on a first draft: A Booth, R Fairley, N J Gordon, P K Kinnear and P Marren and to I Colquhon and R A H Smith for other information. My thanks also go to P Marren and his publishers for permission to quote from his book.

6

Tentsmuir Point: A National Nature Reserve in Decline?

Robert M M Crawford

Introduction

Tentsmuir Point, the north-eastern extremity of an extensive coastal dune and slack system at Tentsmuir, Fife, has been a National Nature Reserve now for over 40 years. It is therefore timely and appropriate to examine whether the managed statutory protection that this status should afford, and the implementation of specific management plans, has had a beneficial or harmful effect on the preservation of biodiversity in this unique coastal site. The Reserve is of special ecological interest as it occupies a relatively undisturbed area of Scottish lowland coastline, with Europe's last major unpolluted waterway – the Tay – to the north and another outstanding biological refuge, the Eden Estuary, to the south. Tentsmuir is an ideal site for a reserve, being undisturbed by industry, other than by forestry, and with agricultural activity confined to the landward side of the forestry plantations. Touristic development has been confined to one picnic area to the south of the Reserve which has also done much to reduce the impact of disturbance in the Reserve at Tentsmuir Point. It has also benefited through the presence of a Ministry of Defence airfield to the south restricting access to part of the coastline.

The location of Tentsmuir Point, with the fortunate provision of a seemingly unending supply of off-shore sand, has produced a landscape that has been growing ever since the end of the last ice age. Present day accretion rates (see pp. 69 and 72 and Chapter 1) appear to be of a similar order of magnitude as those that have operated in the past. The acidic sand is rapidly depleted of mineral nutrients and there is an abrupt fall in soil pH behind the mobile dune systems. This leads to distinct zonation of vegetation parallel to the coast line, as the salt-tolerant species of the seaward regions give way in succession to the plant communities of the fresh-water slacks, grey dunes, dune heath and fresh-water marshes. Interspersed between these communities are extensive areas of alder, birch and willow. The rapidity of coastal accretion, coupled with this prompt evolution of diverse habitats, has created a wealth of sites for colonisation by an extensive flora and diverse invertebrate fauna.

The rapid changes in plant communities across such a small area as Tentsmuir Point is all the more surprising in that the entire biodiversity of the region is supported by the same acid sand-based soil. There are nevertheless physical and chemical differences in the soil which are related to changes in relief, distance from the sea and variation in water-table levels. Moving landward the maritime influence decreases, but the frequency of high water-tables increases due to the obstruction of natural drainage channels by the accreting sand. When two counteracting gradients exist across any terrain the changing ratios of resource availability creates a continually changing environment, varies the impact of competition and creates biodiversity (Tilman 1994) It is the cross gradients of flooding stress, nutrient supply and maritime exposure that are responsible for the wide diversity of habitats that have developed, even on the same sandy soil across the Tentsmuir Reserve (Figs. 6.1–6.2).

In short, the floristic and invertebrate diversity of Tentsmuir does not exist just because the Reserve is an extensive dune and slack system, but is also due to the unique combination of location, topography, drainage, coastal accretion based on relatively shell-free sand, and land-use history. The range of environmental variation is greater moving landwards at this site than can be seen in other Scottish east coast dune systems that have attracted conservation attentions such as Dunnet Bay in Caithness, the Sands of Forvie and St Cyrus. The woodland areas of birch and alder that intersperse the dunes and slacks at Tentsmuir contribute greatly to habitat diversity by creating ecotone zones where many of the rarer species (e.g. *Corallorhiza trifida*) were once able to flourish in profusion and added greatly to the floristic richness of the area.

Tentsmuir Point Before it Became a National Nature Reserve

At the time of the declaration of the Reserve in 1954, the extensive dune and slack system between the two rivers had over 420 recorded species of flowering plants, 320 of which were recorded on the most physically varied and relatively small accreting area to the north which was designated as a reserve. In addition, as shown in Chapter 4, it was a regular breeding ground for Arctic, Common, Little, Sandwich and sometimes Roseate Terns, as well as Eider, Shelduck and Dunlin, and was a site of passage for many migrating birds. However, it should not be construed that Tentsmuir achieved this degree of biological diversity through being either remote or undisturbed. There is both archaeological (see Chapter 2) and place-name evidence that this area of coastal moorland and dune slacks has had a long history of transhumance. The name *Tentismuris* was first recorded in 1476 (Thompson *et al.*, 1882–1914a) and as *Murtoun* (now Morton) *in Tentis muris* in 1529 (Thompson *et al.*, 1882–1914b). This suggests that at this medieval date, Tentsmuir was a recognised site for temporary settlements, most probably for summer graziers. Although these observations are from very differing periods they all indicate that the area has had a long established pastoral use.

Before the small northern area of Tentsmuir Point became an NNR (National Nature Reserve) in 1954, Tentsmuir had had a robust but precarious existence as a grouse moor and duck shoot, and from 1890 was under the management of the Berry family. Dr John Berry has kindly provided the following description *(pers. comm.)* of how the moor was managed before it was taken over by the Forestry Commission in 1924, which includes the time during which it was under his father's control. About 1870, a bad fire, followed by a very severe gale on 17 November 1873, had left an extensive area of drifting sand producing a desert-like appearance – not unlike the Culbin Sands in their earlier treeless condition (although on a smaller scale). There were many very high dunes – over 50 ft high – possibly built up over buried forest trees, together with the remnants of forest and barren moorland. During periods of high tides, salt water penetrated well into the moor where there was a huge

Figure 6.1: The Tentsmuir National Nature Reserve looking north-north-west in 1956 showing the zonation of habitats parallel to the shore-line.
Particularly noticeable is the linear flood-line development of the alder slacks.
(Photo: J K S St Joseph. Crown copyright reserved)

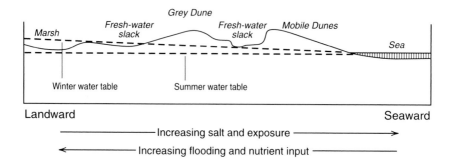

Figure 6.2: Diagrammatic representation of the impact of opposing gradients of maritime influence (salt and exposure) and water-tables levels (flooding and nutrients) in a cross-section of the Tentsmuir Reserve from land to sea (not to scale).
Such opposing gradients create a high degree of habitat differentiation and increase the potential for niche differentiation.

hollow. The influence of high salt concentrations, drought, erosion and flooding, provided a shifting and unstable landscape with much bare ground, generally evoking an impression of great physical fragility. Physical fragility, however, does not imply that the area was in anyway biologically impoverished. The grouse population was low (Berry 1894), but was healthy, and the regular flooding with salt-water protected the birds from infection by *Strongylosis* (Lovat 1911). This disease was then prevalent and a canal was purposely cut to facilitate the salination of the slacks as this was known to reduce the viability of the grouse parasite (Smith 1948). Ditches were dammed wherever possible, primarily to create breeding sites for waterfowl, but also to attract dragonflies and water beetles. Physically, the moor was a place of contrasts, with large dunes and many low-lying wet slacks. Consequently, fresh and salt-water marshes and pools of open fresh water existed in close juxtaposition to areas of waste-land and shifting sands. Botanically, the dominant species over much of the moor was *Calluna vulgaris* with extensive areas of *Salix repens, Vaccinium vitis idaea,* and extensive stands of *Corallorhiza trifida,* as well as numerous sites with *Teesdalia nudicaulis.* Clumps of pine and birch occurred on the southern half of the moor, with the latter providing a valuable habitat for insects, e.g. vapourer moth. The whole area was populated by rabbits with a density of population that justified the employment of two rabbit trappers.

At the beginning of this century we have, therefore, a picture of Tentsmuir, much as it would have been over past centuries, as a place for rough grazing and for sport. Fire, wind-erosion, flooding, and frequent salt deposition all interacted on the physically fragile nature of the sand dune complex and created a diversity of habitats which accommodated a large number of species. In particular, the shifting nature and instability of the sand dune system would have been important in preserving the pioneer species that disappear once dominant, resource demanding, competitive species establish themselves in stable habitats. It was, in effect, the physical fragility of the dune and slack system and its heterogeneity that created the wealth of species which made Tentsmuir the naturalists' delight – which it clearly was at the beginning of this century (Wilson 1910) as was recorded in the journals of many distinguished naturalists, including Edward Wilson of Antarctic fame (Seaver 1935).

This habitat heterogeneity began to disappear when the area landward of the present reserve was purchased by the Forestry Commission in 1924. The planting of trees brought about a reduction in blow outs, and with the implementation of drainage schemes, flooding decreased and the access to salt flooding was impaired (Smith, 1948). However, the continuous accretion to seaward, created new salt slacks and mobile dunes, and this constant provision of new habitat areas preserved much of the biodiversity of the area which was eventually to become an NNR 30 years later.

Tentsmuir Point Becomes a National Nature Reserve

When Tentsmuir Point became an NNR, it was possibly at the height of its ecological diversity, with a dynamic dune and slack system having the highest rate of seaward extension to be found anywhere in the British Isles. The dynamic nature of this accretion was associated with the synergistic action of both *Leymus* (*Elymus*) *arenarius* (Fig. 6.3) and *Ammophila arenaria,* the former species being particularly active in advancing the position of the mobile dunes by the active lateral growth that it can accomplish on the seaward side of dunes. The latter species, *A. arenaria,* consolidates this extension by its capacity for vertical growth and the active manner in which it responds to burial by fresh sand, thus aiding the growth in height of the dunes. Tentsmuir was particularly fortunate in the middle part of this century to have possibly the best population of *Leymus arenarius* in Britain (Ratcliffe 1977). These Fife dunes and slacks and adjacent woodlands were also a unique meeting place for plants from northern and southern floras (Fullerton 1956). A number of arctic species occurring at Tentsmuir are at or near the southern limit of their geographical range, e.g. *Ligusticum scoticum* and *Juncus balticus.* Southern species at the northern limit of their distribution range include, *Centaurium littorale, C. erythraea* and *C. pulchellum, Monotropa hypopitys, Artemisia maritima* and *Dianthus deltoides.* Not only did Tentsmuir provide a refuge for many other uncommon plant species (e.g. *Corallorhiza trifida, Moneses uniflora*), it was also a nesting place for eider duck and terns as well as being a site where many migrating bird species could be seen, including snow buntings and ospreys.

This undisturbed coastline between the rivers Tay and Eden was a veritable conservationist's dream, with no disturbance, no pollution and seemingly no threats to the continuing presence of species which had probably existed there for millennia. The duties of the Nature Conservancy did not appear to be onerous, and it might have been thought that a custodial function ensuring the preservation of the status quo would have been all that was required. In Chapter 5, Huxley records the development of the Nature Conservancy's management plan for Tentsmuir. In the plan it is evident that in the Conservancy's perception the primary interest of the reserve was physiographical, due to the remarkable rate of coastal accretion that was currently being recorded. Short term estimates of accretion rate at the most actively growing point (Fig. 6.4) vary, depending on the time interval over which the accretion is measured (Crawford 1989). In the period between 1940 and 1986, rates depending on position and time interval of as much 7–14 m per annum could be recorded. However, if the rate of accretion is calculated from the site of the Morton

Figure 6.3: Stand of sea lyme grass (*Leymus arenarius*) on the seaward side of a front mobile dune.
At Tentsmuir this species has been particularly active in assisting the recent seaward accretion of the Reserve at its north-eastern extremity.
(Photo: R M M Crawford)

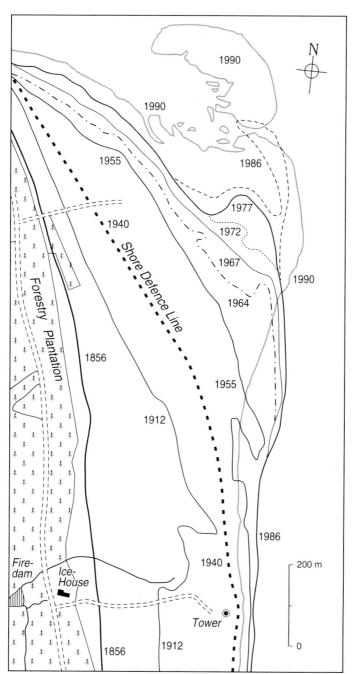

Figure 6.4: Coastal changes between 1856 and 1990 at Tentsmuir National Nature Reserve, reconstructed from charts and Admiralty charts of the Firth of Tay and aerial photographs

Mesolithic investigation (see Chapter 1), which probably represents the coastline *c.* 6000 years before present, then a mean growth rate of approximately 0.8 m per annum is obtained. When averaged over the entire post-glacial period taking the starting point as the Leuchars-Tayport road (GR NO452255) adjacent to the inland cliff face that represents the probable coast line immediately after the retreat of the ice 12,000 years before present, then an average accretion rate approximately 0.5 m per annum is obtained. As the sea has re-advanced over the land at different times over the past 12,000 years, then an average rate of accretion of 7 m per annum, as seen at present, is of the same order of magnitude as that which has probably taken place over the entire Holocene period (Crawford & Wishart 1966). It may have been the impact of this astonishing record of coastal accretion, confirmed by the evidence in Chapter 1, that caused the authors of the first management plan to restrict their interest in the biodiversity of the Reserve to observations of the process of colonisation and succession as the reserve extended its terrain seawards.

Management Plans That Neglected Habitat and Species Diversity

From an ecological point of view the first management plan (1956) makes disappointing reading, as no analysis is presented of how the biodiversity of the Reserve had arisen, or what steps would be necessary for its preservation (see Chapter 5). The main points of the management plan restrict themselves to the objective of (1) 'to retain the area in such a state that changes of coastline etc... and colonisation by vegetation might be studied', (2) 'to measure coastal accretion', and (3) 'encourage ecological and geomorphological studies'. It was also recognised that the area would be prone to tree-invasion from the now maturing forestry plantation to landward and all exotic tree species were to be weeded out of the reserve including all Scots Pine seedlings. The second management plan (1963) still emphasised the importance of Tentsmuir for its physiographic interest, but also noted its botanical importance. Probably this was the period when the flora of Tentsmuir was at its most spectacular, in terms of abundance of flowers, even of the rarer species. The Great Slack was still prone to salt flooding (Fig. 6.5) and preserved a rich halophytic flora. The population of *Corallorhiza trifida* was reputed to be the largest in the British Isles and the mid-summer flowering of the *Centaurium spp.* was one of the unforgettable delights of a visit to the landward side of the mobile dunes. Similarly, the populations of halophytic species *(Juncus gerardii, J. balticus, Glaux maritima)* and profuse blooming in the Great Slack of the Northern marsh orchid (*Orchis purpurella*) was on a scale that has not been evident in recent decades.

The 1963 second management plan confirmed the Nature Conservancy's resolve to manage Tentsmuir as a dune system. Once again no analysis was made of the reasons for the botanical richness of this area, nor was there any appreciation that Tentsmuir was more than just a dune system. The alder slacks, birch woods, marshes and willow stands all contributed to the biodiversity of the area and existed in a state of continual change through succession and forward migration on to new territory. This author was fortunate enough to have shown to him, in a visit in the early 1960s with the late Len Fullerton (local artist and naturalist with an unsurpassed knowledge of the Tentsmuir flora and fauna), the sites of greatest species richness which were at the interfaces between dunes and slacks, alder carr and slack and woodland and grey

Figure 6.5: Aerial view of the Great Slack as photographed in 1963.
Note the absence of trees, the numerous inlets that still permitted salt flooding. The mottled appearance of the ground as seen from the air indicates a wide variety of niche differentiation with dark patches representing the wetter soils covered with a mat of blue-green algae.
(Photo: J K S St Joseph. Crown copyright reserved)

dune. It was the existence of these many ecotones (transition zones) which provided the wealth of habitat variation that lay behind the biodiversity of the Reserve. Unfortunately, cognisance of this important fact was never recorded or discussed in any management plan for the Reserve. Instead, a static policy was developed which declared the area had to be kept as a dune system and measures were to be introduced to restrict the spread of trees onto the reserve. The importance of succession was not considered, and the need for preserving the oligotrophic nature of the dune system was not mentioned until a later management plan (1991), by which time extensive eutrophication had taken place.

Not until the third management plan, produced in 1973, was the question of conserving habitat and species variety discussed, and even this was again subordinated to the prime need of not interfering with the physiographical development of the dune system. The fourth plan in 1991, however, did at last realise that the situation of the dune system and its relatively small size resulted in the Reserve being vulnerable to the effects of adjacent land management, such as drainage, aerial spraying and spread of tree seed. These dangers should have been apparent from the initial creation of the reserve and it is a subject for much regret that in the initial planning this problem was not addressed. However, even more disappointing is the failure in the fourth plan to examine the management strategy that had been in use for the past 35 years and to consider whether the Nature Conservancy's own management policy had been instrumental in contributing to the decline in biodiversity and accelerating the eutrophication of the Reserve that is now all too sadly evident.

Ecological Deterioration and Loss of Biodiversity

1. Pine Invasion

The invasion of pine was an ecological change that was obviously bound to take place, given the proximity of a massive seed source in the adjacent Forestry Commission plantation. Due to the high rabbit population, this did not take place until 1963, when the decimation of the rabbits from myxomytosis enabled the pine seedlings to establish themselves across wide areas of the Reserve which until then had remained relatively treeless, except for stands of willow, alder and birch. The spread of the pine seedlings took off with extraordinary vigour, occupying dunes and slacks right up to rear of mobile dunes (Fig. 6.6). It became evident that Tentsmuir would soon cease to be the dune system that the management plan had decreed should occupy this site in perpetuity. The remedy adopted – first elimination by pulling up saplings and then later clear-felling of what had become a 20 year-old forest – may have appeared the only course available. The felling of the well-established trees was only undertaken after much reflection, as it was feared that the removal of the trees at this stage would leave a landscape subject to further degradation from drought and erosion (see Chapter 5). The question might have been asked as to why pine colonisation had not occurred at an earlier period when it clearly took place very rapidly in the mid-1960s. Seed sources had always been available although obviously not in such quantity. No discussion ever arose, in any of the management plans, as to how the area had been kept treeless in the past. Just removing the trees was not an ecological remedy, as it only removed the symptom of ecological change and did nothing to address the cause of the problem, namely the suitability of the

Figure 6.6: Aerial view looking north-east of the Tentsmuir Reserve, taken in 1972, showing the rapid extension of pine
(Photo: J K S St Joseph. Crown copyright reserved)

habitat for the growth of pine. The role of inundation by fresh as well as salt-water which had been actively encouraged in the past was also not discussed. The lack of blow-outs and the consequent physical stability which now prevailed over large parts of the dune system in a way that had never been possible in previous centuries, was evident. However, adherence to the management plan doctrine – that nothing should be done which would interfere with the natural physiographic development of the area – would probably have inhibited any serious discussion of recreating the level of physical disturbance that prevented tree colonisation in the past. This, in retrospect, is an obvious oversight. Cutting of canals to admit salt-water had been actively encouraged in the early years of this century. There were also areas where fire could have been used to good effect as it would have reduced tree cover and decreased rather than increased eutrophication. A less drastic remedy would have been to thin the forest cover and allow the communities to develop that in the past must have sustained some of the species that have contributed to the floristic interest of Tentsmuir such as *Monotropa hypopitys, Listera cordata* and *L. ovata*. Alternatively, some assistance could have been given to the accretion process so as to facilitate the growth of a new Great Slack. Several times this process has been set back by winter storms. Some transplanting of *Leymus arenarius* and associated colonising species, together with some brushwood protection against erosion, could have aided the recreation of a habitat for the diminished halophytic flora.

2. Birch Invasion

During the removal of the pine trees, it was decided not to eradicate birch growing in the same area, as this species had long been a constituent feature of the Reserve. In the first half of this century the birch was characteristically found to landward of the flood-line alder associations (Fig. 6.7). The latter developed along the edges of the first fresh water slacks to occur to landward of the accreting dune systems as seed, washed into the area, came to rest on the dune edges bordering these slacks where they could germinate without being inhibited by prolonged flooding (McVean 1956). The increased nutrient status that was brought about by the nitrogen fixing properties of the alders, allowed the birches to follow in succession along the landward side of the flood-line alder carr (Fig. 6.7). Any extension of the birch to the rear of this area was limited by the winter flooding of the landward slacks and no invasion to seaward into the Great Slack occurred due to periodic inundation by sea water.

During the period 1970 to 1975 there took place the sudden desalination of the Great Slack, partly due to coastal accretion, but largely as a consequence of an extensive drainage programme carried out by the Forestry Commission in agreement with the Nature Conservancy. The halophytic flora which had been a feeding ground for migrating snow buntings vanished. Monitoring of pH change across the Reserve (Fig. 6.8) showed how rapidly the process of desalination took place, with the zone of high maritime pH retreating seawards by 150 m in under five years (Crawford 1989). The loss of the halophytic flora caused the greatest reduction in biodiversity in the flora of Tentsmuir this century. Although most of the species can still be sought out in residual refugia, the extensive cover of this striking flora with its large populations of salt rushes (*Juncus balticus* and *J. gerardii*) disappeared, and with them the colourful displays of *Armeria maritima, Centaureum erythraea* and *Parnassia palustris*. Salt marsh species, with their characteristic high sugar

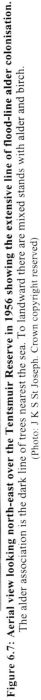

Figure 6.7: Aerial view looking north-east over the Tentsmuir Reserve in 1956 showing the extensive line of flood-line alder colonisation. The alder association is the dark line of trees nearest the sea. To landward there are mixed stands with alder and birch.
(Photo: J K S St Joseph. Crown copyright reserved)

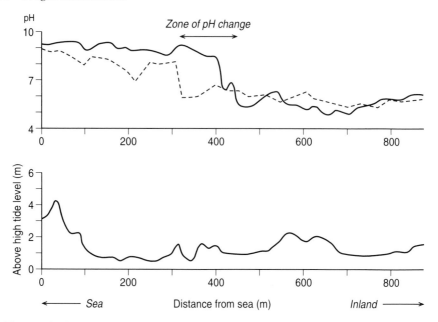

Figure 6.8: Change in pH levels (1970–75) along a transect through the Great Slack at Tentsmuir, running inland from the newly accreted zone.
Note the rapid displacement landwards of the boundary marking the change from high to low pH

concentration for protection against osmotic injury, are particularly nutritious for over-wintering birds, the loss of which is a further regret for the demise of this ecologically important salt slack. In the past, the rapidity of change would have been less and would probably have taken place only after another salt slack had developed to seaward. However, the proximity of the slack to shelter from the forest, the reduction in blow outs and the cessation of the practice of allowing access to salt flooding, coupled with the injudicious decision to agree to an extension of the forest drainage system, caused this spectacular plant community to disappear in a period of 5–10 years, between 1966 and 1976.

The immediate consequence of the desalination of the Great Slack was the rapid invasion of the area with a vast cohort of birch (Fig. 6.9). If this slack had followed the normal successional pattern, it would have passed from one dominated by the halophytic flora to one in which *Salix repens, Juncus balticus, Parnassia palustris* and *Lotus corniculatus* would have been dominant plants and tree growth would have been prevented, as salt flooding would still have been a risk from time to time. The stability of conditions that developed in the Great Slack by 1970 had excluded all salt inundations and there was now no barrier to the establishment of birch. Birch, being a deciduous tree with a well-developed root system, is capable of drawing nutrients upwards from the water-table zone of the soil and increasing the nutrient status of the top soil, which assists the process of eutrophication and destroys the sharp habitat delineations which had been such a marked feature of Tentsmuir and were responsible for its great biodiversity.

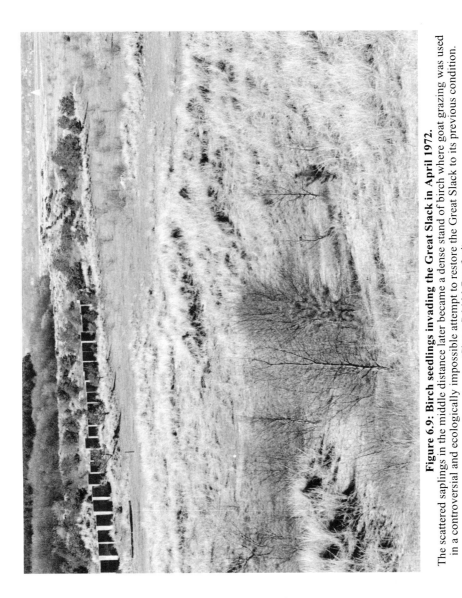

Figure 6.9: Birch seedlings invading the Great Slack in April 1972.
The scattered saplings in the middle distance later became a dense stand of birch where goat grazing was used in a controversial and ecologically impossible attempt to restore the Great Slack to its previous condition.
(Photo: R M M Crawford)

Once again the reaction of the Nature Conservancy was to remove the symptom of the malady and ignore the cause of the disorder. If the objective of the management plan – to plan to preserve the dune and slack system – was to have been adhered to, then immediate steps should have been taken to re-introduce salt flooding to the Great Slack and restore the salt flora before it was extinguished from the area. However, the over-riding priority of non-interference with the physiographic development of the coastline, apparently caused this possibility to be ignored. The remedy that has been attempted – grazing by goats – temporarily reduces the tree cover, but aids the process of nutrient cycling and eutrophication initiated by birch establishment, and ensures that birch will return to the area as soon as the goats are removed. Given the known damage that goats inflict on natural stands of vegetation, this cosmetic attempt to solve the problem of tree colonisation by goat grazing was not only an ecological failure, but arguably an act of ecological vandalism in an area with as many rare species as Tentsmuir.

3. Eutrophication of Rear Slacks and Marshes

The wet-slack and marsh areas immediately adjoining the Forestry Commission plantation also provide a biological indication of the changes that have been brought about in hydrology, resulting from the transpiration needs of the trees and the drainage ditches introduced to reduce the danger of flooding to the plantation. The sand dune system at Tentsmuir is in many ways an unsatisfactory area for tree growth. As already described, the winter rise in water-table levels is greater to landward due to the impedance of drainage by sand accretion limiting the access of streams to the sea. Across the reserve the water-table gradient in early summer from land to sea is approximately 1:400 and this increases in winter. Within the forest itself, the trees reduce the height of the water-table in summer to levels that are too low for species such as sitka spruce and the rising water tables in winter are too high for flood-intolerant pines. There is therefore a constant need for the foresters to avoid excessive winter flooding so that the dominant trees in use, *Pinus sylvestris* and *P. nigra* var. *maritima* do not suffer from winter-flooding injury. Consequently, there has been a greater input of water in winter to those areas of the reserve nearest to the plantation.

Remapping of a dune-slack complex after 24 years, during which it had become subject to increased flooding (Fig. 6.10), provided an opportunity to compare the responses of a number of dune slack communities and their dominant species to a greater flooding frequency with generally higher winter water-tables and increased nutrient supplies. The reaction of the species to longer periods of flooding in the field was compared with laboratory studies of the anoxia tolerance of their perennating organs. In areas where flooding was shallow the anoxia-intolerant *Glyceria maxima* expanded rapidly. Paradoxically, the anoxia-tolerant species *Filipendula ulmaria* retreated as a result of the shallow flooding that favoured *G. maxima*. Examination of the phenology of response to flooding in *Filipendula ulmaria* showed that this species combined tolerance of anoxia with a cessation of shoot extension when flooded. Thus, shallow flooding which neither imposed anoxia on the well aerated rhizomes and roots of *G. maxima,* or inhibited growth was sufficient to inhibit the resumption of growth in the deeper placed rhizomes of *F. ulmaria.* As a result of this differing phenological response to high water-tables, the competitive ability of the

Figure 6.10: Winter flooding which is now becoming increasingly eutrophic as a result of its proximity to forestry drains
(Photo: R M M Crawford)

latter species was reduced, and *Filipendula ulmaria* lost ground to *G. maxima* (Figs. 6.11–6.13). The limits to the spread of *G. maxima* appear to be access to nutrients and sufficient water to support optimal growth, but not so much water that the rhizomes are deprived of oxygen. *Glyceria maxima* is thus affected by extremes in relation to flooding with growth reduced in dry years and also limited by prolonged and deep flooding. It is suggested that if ecological diversity is to be maintained in dune slacks then variation in flooding regime will counteract domination by competitive, nutrient-demanding species such as *Glyceria maxima*.

The net effect of the changes that have taken place in the marshes at Tentsmuir, is again a reduction in biodiversity with monotypic stands of *Glyceria maxima* replacing the more diverse community that was hitherto dominated by *Filipendula ulmaria*, *Hydrocotyle palustris* and *Salix repens*.

Alternative Management Strategies to Preserve Botanical Diversity

Consideration has to be given as to whether there were any available strategies available to the Nature Conservancy and subsequently to Scottish Natural Heritage which would have stopped the wholesale destruction of plant communities that has taken place over the past 40 years. As should have been evident from the outset, the change in vegetation that is taking place in the Reserve results from the proximity of the forestry plantation, the shelter it provides, and the changes it causes to the water regime. The presence of the trees alone will cause summer water-tables to drop further and this will have a serious effect, not so much on the rear slacks where the water-table is naturally nearer the surface (Fig. 6.2), but on the front slacks, where, if the water-table drops more than a metre below the surface in summer, excessive drying out will take place in the surface regions of the soil for the support of communities which are dominated by *Salix repens*. In west coast Scottish sites such sensitivity to water table depth is less likely to exist and *S. repens* can colonise the sides of dunes. However, in the drier climate of the east coast of Scotland, *S. repens* is confined to the level slacks due to its need for the proximity of the water table at less than a metre below the surface. The other effect of the forest and its drainage system is to increase the input of nutrients to the reserve; this has been observed in the increase in nutrient status that has been recorded in the rear slacks over the past 24 years (Studer-Ehrensberger *et al*. 1993).

The only long-term remedy to this problem created by the proximity of the Reserve to the forestry plantation is to increase the distance between the forest and the reserve. Opportunities have presented themselves to implement this solution over the past 40 years but have never been acted upon. There have been periods particularly since the mid 1980s (Fig. 6.14) where there was very active accretion beyond the Great Slack which could have been aided by repairing breaches in the new front line of dunes. This remedial work would have accelerated the replacement of the Great Slack by another, even greater in area. The birch forest could have been allowed to develop on the old Great Slack without the attempt to control it by goat grazing. Instead, a natural salt barrier from the new salt slack would have prevented further extension of birch seawards. This alternative plan was suggested by the present author on a variety of occasions, however it was never implemented (or even considered seriously) as it would have constituted a human interference in the natural

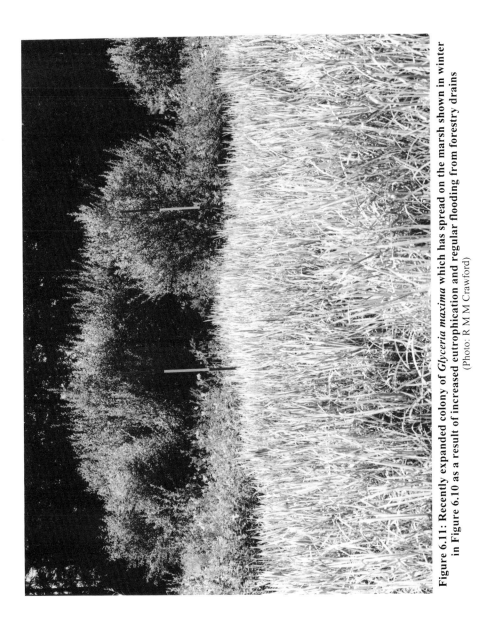

Figure 6.11: Recently expanded colony of *Glyceria maxima* which has spread on the marsh shown in winter in Figure 6.10 as a result of increased eutrophication and regular flooding from forestry drains
(Photo: R M M Crawford)

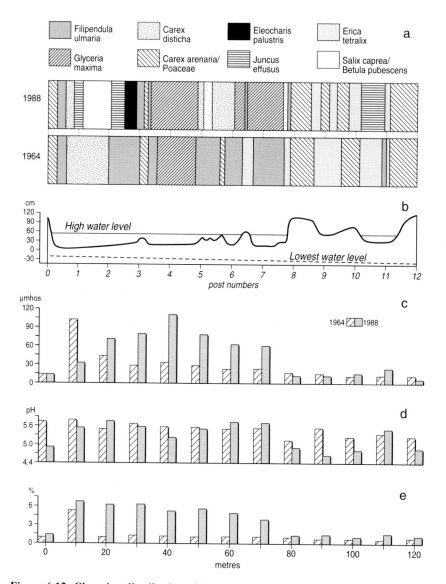

Figure 6.12: Changing distribution of dominant species in the landward fresh water marsh shown in Figures 6.10 and 6.11 in relation to increasing eutrophication; (a) distribution of dominant species in 1988 as compared with 1964, (b) relief, (c) conductivity, (d) pH, (e) organic matter

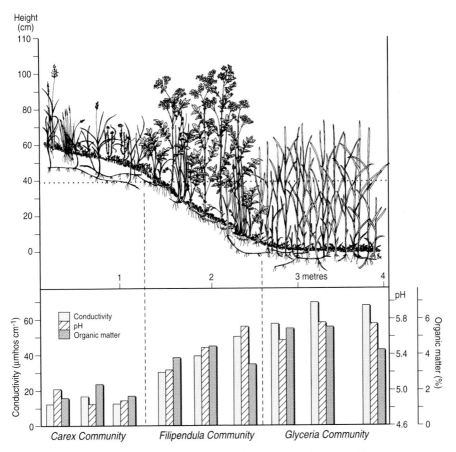

Figure 6.13: Diagrammatic representation of the interface between *Glyceria maxima* and *Filipendula ulmaria* communities in the marsh habitat.

The *F. ulmaria* community has been forced into retreat out of the level ground since 1964 by the *G. maxima* community as a result of increased nutrient-rich flooding.

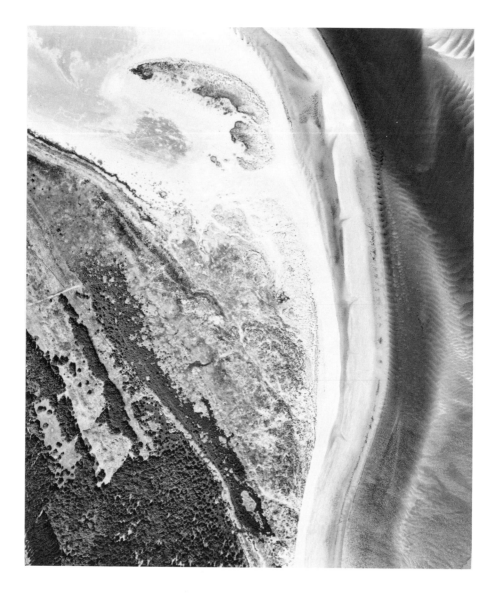

Figure 6.14: Vertical aerial view (1984) showing the new sand-bar that started to grow in the early 1970s at Tentsmuir Point, which, with some assistance from transplanting and brushwood protection, might have been used to advantage to create a new salt slack and protect the diminishing halophytic flora

(Photo: J K S St Joseph. Crown copyright reserved)

process of coastal accretion which has always headed the list of conservation priorities for the Reserve. No argument was ever advanced as to why the process of natural accretion requires further study, and what it was thought might be learnt through passive observation at Tentsmuir. One of the original intentions of setting up National Nature Reserves was for experimentation, and Tentsmuir Point provides a unique opportunity for experiment in recreating the conditions that preserved biodiversity for so long in the past. By paying greater attention to biological processes, much might have been learnt about the creation of habitats and biological diversity and useful information would also have been obtained on how plant communities can accelerate coastal accretion. This latter topic might be considered as of vital importance given the continuing rise in sea levels that is currently taking place.

Conclusions

Tentsmuir Point has to be regarded as a National Nature Reserve in decline, not so much for the absolute loss of any particular species, but for the degradation of landscape in terms of biological interest that has taken place in the last 40 years. An area which once exhibited species-rich communities in abundance, is now in danger of being reduced to a depauperated coastal grassland. The biota that once gave it scientific interest and aesthetic appeal are now reduced to isolated and relict populations that can be seen only after much searching. A policy of expediency, in which the symptoms are attacked but no analysis is made of the underlying causes of change (as in trying to control birch by goat grazing) is not a creditable manner in which to manage a nationally important site, nor is it the proper application of science to an area of much scientific interest. It is still not too late to save the flora of Tentsmuir and restore the biodiversity of its plant communities, provided long-term solutions which attack the cause of the deterioration are used and cosmetic management is abandoned.

Bibliography

Berry, W, 'On the introduction of grouse to the Tentsmuir in Fife', *Annals of Scottish Natural History,* 12 (1894), pp. 197–203

Crawford, R M M, *Studies in Plant Survival* (Blackwell Scientific Publications, Oxford, 1989), p. 296

Crawford, R M M and Wishart, D, 'A multivariate analysis of the development of dune slack vegetation in relation to coastal accretion at Tentsmuir, Fife', *Journal of Ecology,* 54 (1966), pp. 729–43

Fullerton, L, 'Tentsmuir – a changing landscape', *International Union for the Protection of Nature* (Proceedings of Conference, 20–25 June 1956)

Lovat, Simon Joseph Fraser (14th Lord Lovat) (ed.), *The grouse in health and in disease* (2 vols., published for the committee of enquiry on grouse disease by Smith, Elder and Co., London, 1911)

McVean, D N, 'Ecology of *Alnus glutinosa* (L) Gaertn. III. Seedling establishment', *Journal of Ecology,* 44 (1956), pp. 195–218

Ratcliffe, D (ed.), *A nature conservation review* (Cambridge University Press, 1977)

Seaver, G, *Edward Wilson: nature lover* (John Murray, London, 1937), p. 219

Smith, T L, 'Growth and decline of an artificial grouse moor', *The Scottish Naturalist,* 60

(1948), pp. 99–106

Studer-Ehrensberger, K, Studer, C and Crawford, R M M, 'Flood-induced change in a dune slack observed over 24 years', *Functional Ecology* 7 (1993), p. 156–68

Thompson, J M *et al* (eds.), *Registrum Magni Sigilli Regum Scotorum* (The Scottish Record Society, Edinburgh, 1882–1914a, reprinted 1984), vol. 2, no. 1245

Thompson, J M *et al* (eds.), *Registrum Magni Sigilii Regum Scotorum* (The Scottish Record Society, Edinburgh, 1882–1914b, reprinted 1984), vol. 3, no. 760

Tilman, D, 'Competition and biodiversity in spatially structured habitats', *Ecology* 75 (1994), pp. 2–16

Wilson, J H, *Nature study rambles round St Andrews* (W C Henderson and Son, St Andrews, 1910), p. 257

Acknowledgements

I am indebted to Dr John Berry for much information and helpful discussion on the state of Tentsmuir in the late nineteenth and early part of the twentieth centuries and for critically reviewing this paper while in preparation. I am grateful also to Dr Simon Taylor for advice on the earliest recording of Tentsmuir as a place name.

7

Natural Heritage Management of the Sand Dunes of Scotland: Raising Some Issues

Kathy Duncan and Michael B Usher

Introduction

Coastal sand dunes and machair are a distinctive landform and a restricted habitat in Britain, covering approximately 56,000 ha (Doody 1989). The extent and distribution of coastal habitats have been influenced by man's activity over a long period of time so that dune and machair habitats are generally more limited now than they were in the past. In Scotland, however, the dunes and machair have generally been less modified, primarily because of their remoteness. There are therefore still some of the least modified and the most extensive examples of sand dune systems within Britain. Of great importance is the diversity of landforms and the associated high diversity of habitats displayed at these sites. Of particular interest are the extensive dune grasslands or machairs, maintained by grazing and other agricultural activities, which are characteristic of the Western Isles. The distribution of major beach complexes in Scotland is shown in Figure 7.1.

The wildlife on Scottish sand dunes is generally well documented (Dargie 1993; Gimingham 1964; Institute of Terrestrial Ecology 1979; Shaw *et al.* 1983). Both flora and fauna can be extremely rich due to the varied topography and environmental conditions. As an indication of the very high diversity, half the total number of flowering plants that are found in Britain can occur on sand dunes. Not all of these are found in Scotland, as many have a more southerly distribution, but it does demonstrate the potential richness of the sand dune habitats.

The Resource

There are estimated to be approximately 31,400 ha of dune and machair habitat in Scotland (Ritchie & Mather 1984). These were surveyed as part of the Beaches of Scotland study by the Countryside Commission for Scotland between 1969 and 1981. The Beaches survey consisted of a physical inventory of the location, dimensions, morphology, materials, vegetation and land use of the beach complex areas, and it covered all the sand beaches of Scotland, with their associated dunes, links and machair areas. Additional information was recorded concerning ownership and access and particular attention was paid to those aspects of the environment that related to recreation and amenity. This has provided an invaluable reference to the distribution and physical characteristics of the beaches and associated blown sand surfaces.

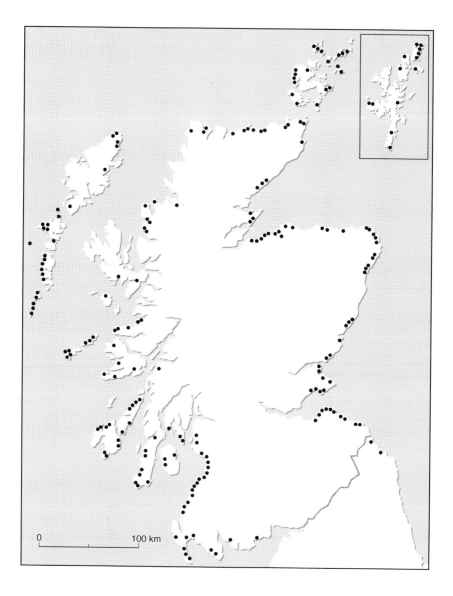

Figure 7.1: Distribution of major beach complexes in Scotland
(after Goudie and Brunsden 1994)

Between 1987 and 1991 a sand dune vegetation survey of Great Britain was carried out by the Nature Conservancy Council. Its objective was to survey the vegetation of sand dune systems in Great Britain using the National Vegetation Classification (NVC) (Dargie 1993; Radley 1994; Dargie 1995). In Scotland 34 sites, which cover approximately 30 percent of vegetated dunes by area (although only about 5 percent of the actual number of dune sites), were surveyed. The location of these sites is shown in Figure 7.2. The sites were chosen to represent the diversity of sand dune vegetation across Scotland. Despite the small sample size, the survey did give a good insight into the nature and diversity of coastal sand dunes and recorded a large habitat diversity. The very large number of NVC communities and subcommunities recorded during the survey illustrates this. Table 7.1 lists the sand dune NVC community and sub-community types found in Britain. In total 38 different NVC sand dune types (out of a British total of 52) and a total of 70 non dune NVC types have been recorded (Dargie 1993). NVC dune communities include strandline, mobile dunes, semi-fixed dunes, dune grassland, slacks and dune scrub. In addition, many non-dune vegetation types are found including heathland and different calcicolous, mesotrophic and acidic grassland communities, woodland, mires or swamp and tall herb fen. There are also transitions to other coastal habitats such as saltmarsh communities and maritime cliff grassland communities. Tentsmuir displays a classic sequence of dune habitats on lime-poor sand from strandline to dune heath with scrub and deciduous woodland. There are also extensive dune slacks which support a diverse flora.

Throughout Great Britain, coastal habitats support 48 nationally rare and 66 nationally scarce plant species (Dargie 1993). Many of these, however, are rare or scarce because they are at the northern or western limit of their range and are therefore predominantly found further south. In Scotland, there are only five nationally scarce dune plant species (i.e. occurring in between 16 and 100 of the 10 x 10 km squares of the national grid); they are seaside centaury *(Centaurium littorale)*, variegated horsetail *(Equisetum variegatum)*, rush-leaved fescue *(Festuca juncifolia)*, baltic rush *(Juncus balticus)* and curved sedge *(Carex maritima)*.

To obtain a full inventory of the Scottish dune resource, an additional vegetation survey is currently being carried out by Scottish Natural Heritage. Over a three and a half year period, this will enable each site to be put into a national context. It should also make it possible to identify and interpret geographical patterns across Scotland and will greatly increase the value of the existing survey data on sand dunes.

Sand dunes and machair support a characteristic fauna. It is recognised that a high diversity of invertebrates can occur, particularly within dune slacks and older dunes. Although this is still a relatively unstudied group, the sequence of different dune habitats, ranging from the open structure of the foredunes through to older dunes with a complete vegetation cover, is critical for characteristic species of insects and molluscs. Sand dunes in the south west of Scotland are also important for the natterjack toad *(Bufo calamita)* which is protected under the Wildlife and Countryside Act (1981).

Managing the Natural Heritage

Scottish Natural Heritage was established in April 1992 through the merger of the Countryside Commission for Scotland and the Nature Conservancy Council for

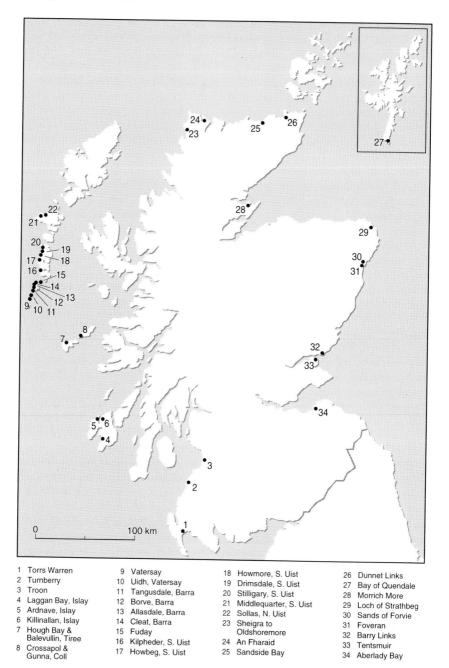

1	Torrs Warren	9	Vatersay	18	Howmore, S. Uist	26	Dunnet Links
2	Turnberry	10	Uidh, Vatersay	19	Drimsdale, S. Uist	27	Bay of Quendale
3	Troon	11	Tangusdale, Barra	20	Stilligary, S. Uist	28	Morrich More
4	Laggan Bay, Islay	12	Borve, Barra	21	Middlequarter, S. Uist	29	Loch of Strathbeg
5	Ardnave, Islay	13	Allasdale, Barra	22	Sollas, N. Uist	30	Sands of Forvie
6	Killinallan, Islay	14	Cleat, Barra	23	Sheigra to	31	Foveran
7	Hough Bay &	15	Fuday		Oldshoremore	32	Barry Links
	Balevullin, Tiree	16	Kilpheder, S. Uist	24	An Fharaid	33	Tentsmuir
8	Crossapol &	17	Howbeg, S. Uist	25	Sandside Bay	34	Aberlady Bay
	Gunna, Coll						

Figure 7.2: Location of sand dunes and machair sites surveyed as part of the sand dune Vegetation Survey of Great Britain

(after Dargie, 1993)

Table 7.1: Sand dune National Vegetation Classification communities and sub-communities, including two provisional types identified during the Sand Dune Vegetation Survey of Great Britain (bold type denotes those found in Scotland)

NVC Community Type		NVC Sub-Community Type
SD2	*Honkenya peploides-Cakile maritima* **strandline**	
SD3	*Matricaria maritima-Galium aparine* **strandline**	
SD4	*Elymus farctus* **ssp** *borealis-atlanticus* **foredune**	
SD5	*Leymus arenarius* **mobile dune**	SD5a species poor sub-community
		SD5b *Elymus farctus* **sub-community**
		SD5c *Festuca rubra* **sub-community**
SD6	*Ammophila arenaria* **mobile dune**	SD6a *Elymus farctus* **sub-community**
		SD6b *Elymus farctus-Leymus arenarius* **sub-community**
		SD6c *Leymus arenarius* **sub-community**
		SD6d **typical sub-community**
		SD6e *Festuca rubra* **sub-community**
		SD6f *Poa pratensis* **sub-community**
		SD6g *Carex arenaria* **sub-community**
SD7	*Ammophila arenaria-Festuca rubra* **semi fixed dune**	SD7a **typical sub-community**
		SD7b *Hypnum cupressiforme* **sub-community**
		SD7c *Ononis repens* **sub-community**
		SD7d *Tortula ruralis* **ssp** *ruraliformis* **sub-community**
		SD7e *Elymus pycnanthus* sub-community
		SD7?f *Galium verum* **sub-community (provisional)**
		SD7?g *Heracleum sphondylium* **sub-comm. (provisional)**
SD8	*Festuca rubra-Galium verum* **fixed dune grassland**	SD8a **typical sub-community**
		SD8b *Luzula campestris* **sub-community**
		SD8c *Tortula ruralis* **ssp** *ruraliformis* **sub-community**
		SD8d *Bellis perennis-Ranunculus acris* **sub-community**
		SD8e *Prunella vulgaris* **sub-community**
SD9	*Ammophila arenaria-Arrhenatherum elatius* **dune grassland**	SD9a **typical sub-community**
		SD9b *Geranium sanguineum* sub-community
SD10	*Carex arenaria* **dune**	SD10a *Festuca rubra* **sub-community**
		SD10b *Festuca ovina* **sub-community**
SD11	*Carex arenaria-Cornicularia aculeata* **community**	SD11a *Ammophila arenaria* **sub-community**
		SD11b *Festuca ovina* **sub-community**
SD12	*Carex arenaria-Festuca ovina-Agrostis capillaris* **grassland**	SD12a *Anthoxanthum odoratum* **sub-community**
		SD12b *Holcus lanatus* **sub-community**
SD13	*Salix repens-Bryum pseudotriquetrum* **dune slack**	SD13a *Poa annua-Hydrocotyle vulgaris* sub-community
		SD13b *Holcus lanatus-Festuca rubra* **sub-community**
SD14	*Salix repens-Campylium stellatum* **dune slack**	SD14a *Carex serotina-Drepanocladus sendtneri* **sub-community**

	SD14b *Rubus caesius-Galium palustre* sub-community
	SD14c *Bryum pseudotriquetrum-Aneura pinguis* sub-community
	SD14d *Festuca rubra* sub-community
SD15 *Salix repens-Calliergon cuspidatum* dune slack	SD15a *Carex nigra* sub-community
	SD15b ***Equisetum variegatum* sub-community**
	SD15c *Carex flacca-Pulicaria dysenterica* sub-community
	SD15d *Holcus lanatus-Angelica sylvestris* sub-community
SD16 *Salix repens-Holcus lanatus* dune slack	SD16a *Ononis repens* sub-community
	SD16b *Rubus caesius* sub-community
	SD16c *Prunella vulgaris-Equisetum variegatum* sub-community
	SD16d ***Agrostis stolonifera* sub-community**
SD17 *Potentilla anserina-Carex nigra* dune slack	SD17a *Festuca rubra-Ranunculus repens* sub-community
	SD17b *Carex flacca* sub-community
	SD17c ***Caltha palustris* sub-community**
	SD17d ***Hydrocotyle vulgaris-Ranunculus flammula* sub-commmunity**
SD18 *Hippophaë rhamnoides* scrub	SD18a ***Festuca rubra* sub-community**
	SD18b ***Urtica dioica-Arrhenatherum elatius* sub-community**

Scotland. The remit of this new organisation is to secure the conservation and enhancement of the natural heritage of Scotland, and to help people to understand, enjoy and use it wisely so that it can be sustained for future generations. SNH, therefore, has a perspective that is wider than pure nature conservation and hence its approach to the sand dunes of Scotland has to be holistic in nature.

Conservation of the Natural Heritage

Traditionally SNH and other conservation organisations have concentrated on the protection of those sites that contain the best examples of habitats, communities, landforms and rock sequences. These are designated as, for example, Sites of Special Scientific Interest (SSSI) and National Nature Reserves (NNR). Management of these sites has tended to concentrate on maintaining the existing interest for which the site was designated. Many habitats, and in particular coastal habitats such as dune systems, are naturally dynamic, continuing to evolve under the changing climatic and physical processes that influence them. It is therefore debatable whether coastal managers should be carrying out active management in order to maintain existing interests or whether they should be allowing natural succession to take place, therefore allowing the interest to change over time. This raises all sorts of issues relating to colonisation of dune systems by non-native or non-local species such as seeding in from adjacent plantations of Scots Pine (*Pinus sylvestris*) or other tree species.

In the past there was concern that sand dunes were too mobile and therefore vulnerable to erosion. Numerous attempts were made in Scotland to stabilise the ground by, for example, carrying out large-scale afforestation schemes, planting sea buck-thorn or building fences. Many of these methods were successful but increasingly it is being recognised that natural erosion is an intrinsic element of dune systems and that this type of management is not beneficial in the long-term to the natural heritage interests. Indeed, it will often be detrimental to the diversity of species, habitats and landforms. For example, the extensive afforestation that has been carried out at Tentsmuir and at Culbin on the Moray coast, for timber production, has resulted in stabilisation of the site and loss of natural coastal habitat.

With greater knowledge of the sedimentary and hydrodynamic processes mould-ing our coastline, SNH recognises that the continuation of these processes is essential for the overall health of the coastline. The effects of limiting the sediment movement in one area may have severe consequences elsewhere. Coastal systems follow natural cycles of erosion and stabilisation that are beyond our ability to control and to which we can only adapt.

In recent years it has been recognised that the coastline may be sub-divided into more or less discrete units or 'coastal cells' (Fig. 7.3) within which the sediment transport processes are inter-related. Each 'cell' is a self-contained stretch of coast-line in which the processes of erosion and accretion are interdependent. Any process or operation influencing sediment transport within one part of the cell, such as the construction of coastal protection, will thus affect other areas within that cell but not the coastline outwith the cell. Within each cell the principal direction(s) and magni-tude of littoral drift may be established and areas of long term erosion or accretion identified. SNH, in partnership with the Scottish Office Environment Department and Historic Scotland, has funded a research project to identify the location of these cells around the Scottish coastline, encompassing virtually all of the most valuable dune systems. The identification of these makes it easier to determine the signifi-cance and distribution of any effects upon coastal sediment transport, and resultant beach or dune formation, which a proposed construction or operation may have.

As sedimentary processes can extend over large areas, beyond the boundaries of SSSIs, the major influences on a coastal site can often originate from an activity fur-ther along the coast where the designation has no control over what activities are car-ried out. With the identification of coastal cells it is easier to predict these types of changes and effects. It also indicates how important it is to manage the coastal zone as a whole, rather than restricting protection to individual sites. This argues for a more holistic and integrated approach to managing the coastal natural heritage of Scotland.

Where significant changes on dune systems are a result of natural processes, it is accepted that change will happen. However, there are many areas that are disturbed or damaged as a result of human activity and in these cases it is beneficial to manage the site to minimise the impact and maintain the conservation interest. Human activ-ity is widespread on Scottish dunes, although its intensity is much less than on the dunes in England and Wales. Of particular importance is the impact of agriculture, forestry, industrial development, recreation and the development of golf courses. However, there are also military training operations and sand extraction; all of these forms of land use have varying levels of impact. In many cases – even if the sand dunes are not directly modified – if the area landward has been developed or influenced, transitional habitats are lost. With coastal erosion occurring on the seaward side as well, dune habitats are often squeezed as they are unable to migrate

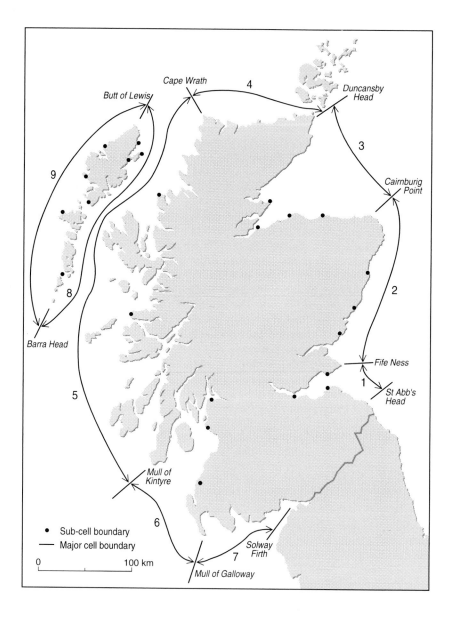

Figure 7.3: Location of major coastal cells and sub-cells in Scotland, excluding Orkney and Shetland

landwards and the overall extent of sand dunes is reduced.

One of the main areas of activity for SNH is working with owners and occupiers to encourage an appropriate management regime that is beneficial to the special interest of that site. It is often not possible (or desirable) to exclude people and their activities from the site, but it is possible to reduce conflict by ensuring that management is more environmentally sensitive. Management is not only more effective but often, in the long run, cheaper if the natural processes are not interfered with. Therefore, in providing management advice to owners and occupiers of the shore, to regulators or to other authorities in the coastal zone, SNH advocates working with the natural processes, as far as possible.

Traditionally coastal dune areas have been used for low intensity agriculture and, in particular, grazing of stock. In the Western Isles, traditional management of machair results in a large habitat and species diversity. However, modern methods using fertilisers and pesticides, and increasing stock density, are having a detrimental effect on many of these sites. Grazing, either by rabbits or by stock (sheep and cattle) or both, is universal on most dune systems. The level at which grazing occurs is the important factor in determining whether it is beneficial or damaging. Over-grazing will result in erosion and loss of species diversity; however, under-grazing can also be detrimental to sites that have traditionally been grazed. In these cases, tall rank grasslands and scrub can develop taking over from the original species-rich dune grassland. It is necessary to look at each site on its own, taking into account past grazing regimes, the size of the site and the vegetation structure, in order to set optimum grazing levels, recognising that the optimum may vary from year to year, due, for example, to annual variation in temperature and precipitation. At Tentsmuir goats have been introduced and their grazing regime carefully managed in order to control birch scrub which has invaded large areas of the NNR, but superficial observation indicates that the goats may prefer willow (*Salix repens*).

Enhancement of the Natural Heritage

There is potential for enhancing degraded habitats and species within the coastal environment. Recovery and restoration are positive approaches that can reverse past damage and improve the natural balance and productivity of an area.

Sand dunes are naturally mobile and, in this state, support the greatest diversity of habitats with their associated species, and are of great interest geomorphologically. Many systems have already been stabilised by, for example, building coast protection and sea defences to stop erosion or by planting vegetation. Restoration of sites to their original state should be encouraged wherever feasible by removing these artefacts, or allowing them to degenerate, and restoring the natural sediment dynamics. This will not always be possible where, for example, coast protection is adjacent to urban land, but in many other areas where pressure is less it can be encouraged. Is coastal set-aside a viable option?

Extensive restoration works have been carried out on sand dunes in an attempt to prevent or reduce erosion that is a result of both man-made activities and natural processes. Over the years considerable experience has been gained by both SNH and others in the maintenance, protection and repair of vulnerable coastal environments. These include techniques such as regrading, replanting of dune grasses, mulching, thatching and use of fences to trap sand.

Species recovery projects have been carried out in Scotland (for example the sea eagles, *Haliaetus albicilla*, re-introduction programme) and considerable work has gone into studying the population distribution of other species, for example the endemic Scottish primrose (*Primula scotica*). In most cases, however, there is a lack of knowledge about where restoration is needed, and the management needed to achieve it. Vulnerable species and habitats need to be identified and appropriate techniques adopted to encourage their recovery. High profile recovery programmes of species or sites are also an effective way of increasing awareness among others of both SNH's work and the value of the natural heritage. SNH's Species Action Programme aims to maintain or restore viable populations of threatened or declining native species within their traditional range. It is intended to meet commitments within the UK Biodiversity Action Plan (Anon 1994) and there will be opportunities in the future to extend the list to cover other species.

Enjoyment of the Natural Heritage

Being popular places to visit, coastal areas often come under severe pressure from recreation. On average over twelve million day trips are made to the Scottish coast each year, with 50 percent of these being to undeveloped areas where there are no facilities. Informal activities such as walking, picnicking, camping and birdwatching tend to have a low impact (except upon shore nesting birds) but, if at a high enough level, may require car parking and other facilities. Other activities such as mountain biking, the increasing use of trial bikes and buggies, and perhaps pony trekking, may cause greater disturbance and damage. The scale of damage obviously relates to local conditions and the level of activity, but can include destabilisation and erosion of the dunes leading to loss of vegetation and blow outs. Even walking, resulting in erosion of footpaths along dune ridges, can cause damage particularly when aggravated by trial bikes and other wheeled vehicles. On dune grassland and machair severe damage can be caused by car wheels tearing the vegetation mat, and this may either take many seasons to recover or precipitate deflation or blow out formation.

It is important to highlight the possible areas of conflict between recreational and conservation uses and to demonstrate the need for management of the coastal zone that can integrate recreation with nature conservation and other interests. Part of SNH's remit is to encourage the responsible enjoyment of the natural heritage and as a consequence SNH recently published a policy paper on access to the countryside (SNH 1994). Should there be general access to the coastal zone for the public for recreation, allowing visitors freedom to roam wherever they want? This surely again relates to integrated management, which aims to accommodate all activities through consensus and agreement.

Within the coastal zone, SNH needs to be aware of potential conflicts and solutions to these conflicts as well as potential opportunities where environmentally sensitive enjoyment can be promoted. In many coastal areas there are already existing measures or strategies that do manage the human resource so as to reduce damage resulting from recreational activities. This can be accomplished by zoning the various interests in a site and producing information to inform visitors of both the vulnerability of the site and the reasons behind management. On many sites it will be necessary to formalise the facilities by, for example, providing car parking facilities in one place in order to prevent impacts over a larger area. There are considerable opportunities for SNH in this area to increase people's awareness of the importance and vulnerability of coastal sites which can be achieved through effective site inter-pretation and environmental education. An example of such work is at St Cyrus NNR.

Discussion

Attitudes towards management of the coast have changed dramatically in recent years. We have moved away from the idea of stabilising the coast and thinking that we can preserve sites as they are. Instead, there is a general recognition that coastal sites are naturally dynamic and that this dynamism is part of, and is responsible for, the scientific interest of the site. By inhibiting the natural processes, the naturalness of the site is lost and there is a reduction in both the nature conservation and the landscape interest.

Individual sand dune sites can be protected through the range of mechanisms, such as SSSIs, NSAs, NNRs and, in the future, Special Areas of Conservation. Within these sites SNH continues to work with others to ensure good management of the natural heritage and the protection of the nature conservation and landscape in-terest. Such sites are also areas that can be used to increase awareness among others of the importance and vulnerability of the coast and to demonstrate the benefits of effective management.

It is recognised, however, that coastal habitats can no longer be looked at in isola-tion. Traditional methods of site designation, although beneficial for protecting se-lected areas of coast, cannot fully take into account the highly dynamic nature of the coastal zone. Designation therefore cannot provide comprehensive protection. Instead it is becoming increasingly obvious that the coastal zone must also be man-aged in an integrated fashion. Within the coastal zone there is a huge and very di-verse number of activities being carried out by an equally diverse range of organisa-tions, individuals and regulatory bodies. Not all of these affect the sand dunes di-rectly. Because of the inter-related nature of the coastal and marine environment, es-pecially within coastal cells, influences and changes in one area or habitat may well have consequences elsewhere. Sand dunes can therefore be indirectly affected, some-times quite markedly, by, for example, coastal protection works a long way from the dune system. Recognition of the inter-related nature of all of the components in the coastal cell is important for a more holistic view of any coastal site.

Both in this country and overseas, there is a trend towards looking at integrated management and multiple-use zoning as a solution to reducing conflict within the coastal zone. At present, regulation of activities within the coastal zone is piecemeal and sectoral. To overcome this SNH is increasingly adopting a voluntary approach that encourages integrated management. This is best demonstrated by SNH's Focus on Firths project, which was developed as a consequence of increasing development pressures within estuaries and has become an integral part of the UK Biodiversity Action Plan. At present Focus on Firths has project officers covering three firths, namely the Moray Firth, Solway Firth and Firth of Forth. There is also an SNH pro-ject officer covering the Minch. In these areas SNH is trying to promote integrated management of the natural resources by stimulating understanding, co-operation and voluntary agreement among the range of users and statutory authorities by the creation of local forums. These represent all interested parties, including local government and industry, and will therefore have considerable influence over future development and activity in that area.

Therefore, the management of individual sand dunes is important, but it is also essential to look at any system as part of a much larger coastal zone rather than simply in isolation. On one side it is important that we protect individual dune sites to ensure the maintenance or enhancement of the natural heritage interest. As shown in Chapter 5, Tentsmuir NNR management has involved clear-felling areas of naturally seeded forest to restore sand dune habitats and goats have been introduced to control birch scrub. In addition, however, we must consider the management of the much larger coastal zone within which particular sites lie and promote the concept of integrated management. The importance of this can also be demonstrated by looking at Tentsmuir where the accretion of sand to form embryonic dunes at the northern end shows the influence of sediment processes along the whole stretch of coast extending beyond Tentsmuir. There is also potential conflict between the range of other users and interests.

It is necessary to put considerable effort into increasing awareness of the vulnerability of the coastal zone and promoting its integrated management. Working with others, it will be possible to address all the issues and activities being carried out in the coastal zone and develop management strategies which will help to reduce conflict, while at the same time incorporate all the varying uses of the coastal zone. Of prime concern to SNH is whether this approach will maintain, or even increase, the natural heritage of the Scottish coastline.

Bibliography

Anon., *Biodiversity, the UK Action Plan* (HMSO, London, 1994)

Dargie, T C D, *Sand dune vegetation survey of Great Britain. Part 2 – Scotland* (Joint Nature Conservation Committee, Peterborough, 1993)

Dargie, T C D, *Sand dune vegetation survey of Great Britain. Part 3 – Wales* (Joint Nature Conservation Committee, Peterborough, 1995)

Doody, J P, 'Conservation and development of the coastal dunes in Great Britain', *Perspectives in coastal dune management,* eds. van der Meulen, F, Jungerius, P E and Visser, J H (SPB Academic Publishing, The Hague, 1989), pp. 53–67

Gimingham, C H, 'Maritime and submaritime communities', *The Vegetation of Scotland,* ed. Burnett, J H (Oliver & Boyd, Edinburgh, 1964), pp. 67–142

Goudie, A S and Brunsden, D, *The environment of the British Isles: an atlas* (Clarendon Press, Oxford, 1994)

Institute of Terrestrial Ecology, *The invertebrate fauna of dune and machair sites in Scotland* (Nature Conservancy Council, Peterborough, 1979), CST report 255

Radley, G P, *Sand dune vegetation survey of Great Britain. Part 1 – England* (Joint Nature Conservation Committee, Peterborough, 1994)

Ritchie, W and Mather, A S, *The beaches of Scotland* (Countryside Commission for Scotland, Perth, 1984)

Scottish Natural Heritage, *Enjoying the Outdoors: a Programme for Action* (Scottish Natural Heritage, Battleby, 1994)

Shaw, M W, Hewett, D G and Pizzey, J M, *Scottish coastal survey: a report on soft coast sites in Scotland* (Institute of Terrestrial Ecology, Bangor, 1983)

Acknowledgement

The authors would like to acknowledge the advice of Dr George Lees on the geomorphological aspects of this chapter.

Appendix 1

Tentsmuir Forest Design Plans

N Hugh Clayden

The 1600 ha Tentsmuir Forest is typical of the pine plantations established on littoral sands in Britain during the period 1920–1940. Created primarily with the objectives of stabilising sand dunes and producing timber, these forests have, nevertheless, developed their own unique characteristics.

As Tentsmuir reaches 'economic maturity', its full potential to provide multi-purpose benefits is being developed by Forest Enterprise through the interdisciplinary process of Forest Design Planning. By careful management of the scale, shape and sequence of felling, coupled with the design and composition of the successor crop, the *plantation* of yesterday is being transformed into the more diverse *forest* of the twenty-first century.

The Forest Design Plan for Tentsmuir will:
1. Define clear forest objectives.
2. Resolve conflicts.
3. Enable Forest Enterprise to plan ahead and identify the consequences of decisions.
4. Optimise the productive and environmental potential of the forest.
5. Provide a secure foundation for integrated management and marketing decisions.
6. Produce a coherent and manageable forest structure which is demonstrably better than the previous structure.

The key stages in the preparation of the Forest Design will be:
1. Appraising sensitivity (wildlife, landscape, recreation, water quality, heritage).
2. Ranking objectives (notably timber production, recreation, landscape and conservation).
3. Collating information (cross-referenced, for example, to data on growing stock, recreation plans, the Forest District Conservation Plan, SSSI Management Plans and existing Timber Production forecasts).
4. Appraising felling options (including, practically, meeting market commitments, visual and physical impacts, financial appraisals). A 40–50 year time frame is normally used to provide a strategic context against which the shorter-term (five year) proposals can be viewed.
5. Appraising replanting options (including species choice, natural regeneration vs direct planting, open space requirements, financial appraisal). Again the long term 'vision' is appraised as a strategic context for the first five year period of the Plan.

During the preparation of the Forest Design Plan, advice is sought from a range of organisations and individuals. These include the statutory consultees (see below) and, crucially, the Fife Environment Panel. The latter is a group of individuals, with a range of skills and knowledge, which offers advice to Forest Enterprise on environmental matters. Included in the Panel is a strong Community Council presence.

On completion of the Plan, it will be submitted to the Forestry Authority at which time formal consultation will commence. This involves statutory consultation with the Regional Council and Scottish Natural Heritage (SSSIs). A range of other bodies is also notified as appropriate – either by the Forestry Authority or the statutory consultees.

Provided there are no objections raised and sustained by the statutory consultees, the Forestry Authority will, in due course, issue formal approval for the first five year period of the Forest Design Plan. On receipt of that approval Forest Enterprise can then commence the detailed planning and execution of the agreed Plan, the latter being monitored by the Forestry Authority throughout the five year period.

Every five years the Forest Design Plan will be carefully reviewed, re-appraised and then re-submitted to the Forestry Authority. By this means, the long term future of Tentsmuir Forest will continue to meet the needs of future generations.

Appendix 2

Statutory Sites for Nature Conservation in the Tentsmuir Area

Site Name	Status
Earlshall Muir	Notified as a Site of Special Scientific Interest in 1955. Renotified in 1983 with a reduction of 96 ha (432 ha).
Eden Estuary	Notified as a Site of Special Scientific Interest in 1971. Declared a Local Nature Reserve in 1978 (1161 ha). Renotified as a Site of Special Scientific Interest in 1990.
Morton Lochs	Declared a National Nature Reserve 1952 (24 ha). Renotified in 1983 as part of a larger Morton Site of Special Scientific Interest (49.6 ha).
St Michael's Wood	Notified as a Site of Special Scientific in 1971 (104 ha). Renotified in 1983.
Tentsmuir Point	Declared a National Nature Reserve in 1954. Extended to include the foreshore and Abertay Sands in 1962 (448 ha). Renotified as part of Tayport-Tentsmuir Coast Site of Special Scientific Interest in 1983 (1048 ha).

Index